I Wish
My Teacher Knew

I Wish My Teacher Knew

How One Question Can Change Everything for Our Kids

Kyle Schwartz

hachette
BOOKS

New York

Previously published by Da Capo Lifelong 2016
First Hachette Go edition 2021

Hachette Go, an imprint of Hachette Books
Hachette Book Group
1290 Avenue of the Americas
New York, NY 10104
HachetteGo.com
Facebook.com/HachetteGo
Instagram.com/HachetteGo

Hachette Books is a division of Hachette Book Group, Inc.
The Hachette Go and Hachette Books name and logos are trademarks of Hachette Book Group, Inc.

The publisher is not responsible for websites (or their content) that are not owned by the publisher.

Library of Congress Control Number: 2016010208
ISBN 978-0-7382-1914-1 (hardcover)
ISBN 978-0-7382-1915-8 (ebook)

Note: The information in this book is true and complete to the best of our knowledge. This book is intended only as an informative guide for those wishing to know more about health issues. In no way is this book intended to replace, countermand, or conflict with the advice given to you by your own physician. The ultimate decision concerning care should be made between you and your doctor. We strongly recommend you follow his or her advice. Information in this book is general and is offered with no guarantees on the part of the authors or Hachette Go. The authors and publisher disclaim all liability in connection with the use of this book.

Editorial production by Christine Marra, Marrathon Production Services.
www.marrathon.net

Book design by Jane Raese
Set in 10.5-point Caslon 224

Printed in the United States of America

LSC-C

Printing 16, 2021

I would like to dedicate this book to my students who continue to teach me everyday.

Contents

Author's Note

I Wish My Teacher Knew wouldn't exist without the hundreds of children that I've had the pleasure to teach. Their stories are what make this book come alive. To protect the privacy of my students and their families, certain names and identifying characteristics have been changed.

Introduction

Doull Elementary is not much different from schools across America. Our sixty-year-old school wraps around a hundred-year-old oak tree. On the south side of our building is a wide green baseball field. To the east are a soccer field and a vibrant community garden where the kindergarten students plant pumpkins and neighbors grow corn, cabbage, and sunflowers. Embedded into our sidewalk are metal plaques that list facts about each planet in the solar system, and our playground is capped with a plastic, gray climbing wall that looks like a rock formation. Our school is full of professionals who dedicate themselves to building on our students' strengths and meeting our community's needs.

Every morning, families who love their children and who value education struggle to wake up sleepy students and send them off to school. School bells ring and doors fling open to let in eager students. There is a stampede of feet rushing up the stairs and busy hands scramble to hang up their coats.

Just like at every school, each day my students bring so much more than just their backpacks to school. There is no magic device that separates the troubles and joys of their home life as they walk through our doors. Each student brings a lifetime of memories, thoughts, and feelings. As teachers we need to honor this. We must recognize how these widely diverse experiences shape our students and impact their academic development.

Our school community is strong, but we face challenges—challenges that are all too familiar to many schools in America.

During the 2013–14 school year, 90 percent of our students lived in poverty. More than half of our students speak a language other than English at home. In my own classroom during the 2015–16 school year, about one-third of my students qualify to receive special education services. There are many schools, nationwide, with similar statistics.

As teachers, we can sometimes become overwhelmed by the very real challenges our students face. But it's equally important to remember our students' strengths. We should place equal value on their interests and curiosities, because these passions can motivate our students to become engaged learners. As educators, it is our responsibility to empathize with the realities our students face and understand how those realities impact their learning. By leveraging the resources within our communities, we can work to remove barriers that hamper our students' ability to learn.

There is only one way to do this. It is to form relationships with our students and actively build strong communities inside our classrooms. As educators, we are teaching more than subjects and concepts; we are teaching people. James Comer, a leading child psychiatrist once said, "No significant learning occurs without a significant relationship." Therefore, as a teacher who is primarily responsible for learning, I am also in the business of relationship building.

The most important thing I do in my classroom is to actively build community. Without that, true, passionate, joyful learning is a hard goal to achieve. I do this by creating relationships with my students and their families. I make sure that they feel cared about and heard.

Building community begins the very first second I see my students. I show up every day to teach an amazing group of third graders. I clap words into syllables, I collect field trip forms and picture money, and I try to make sure Ali doesn't pour glue on Julia's head . . . again. I make sure to greet my students each morning by saying, "I'm so glad you are here" and "I care about you, do you believe me?"

One day a student responded, "Ugh . . . yes, I know you care about me. You tell me that all the time!" That was the best eye roll I've ever gotten as a teacher! Creating a sense of community continues throughout the school day. It is in the comfortable seats I provide for my students. It happens when I hand them a book I know they will love or show my genuine thrill that a yellow belt in karate was finally earned. It is in the way I comfort them when they are hurt and laugh at inside jokes we share.

There are a million little ways that I actively build community in my classroom. As you read this book, I am sure you will realize that there are a million little ways you do this in your classrooms and offices every day too. Much to my surprise, one of the little ways I built community went "viral." It was a simple exercise: I asked a question and listened for the answer.

As a first-year teacher, I worried about how much I didn't know about my students. I explained to them that I wanted to get to know them better. I wrote, *"I wish my teacher knew . . ."* on the board and asked them to complete the sentence.

Each student's response was unique. They responded with honesty, humor, and vulnerability. Sometimes their notes talked about their favorite sport. Sometimes students complained about conflict with siblings or friends. They wrote about their home life and the people who meant most to them. Sometimes they articulated their hopes for the future and sometimes they explained obstacles they were facing. After completing this lesson, I was amazed at how well it helped me connect with my students. Their notes became a tangible reminder for me to truly listen to the voices of students in my classroom.

It was always a meaningful lesson for me, but the problem was that the power of the lesson stayed inside Room 207. I did not share the idea with my colleagues. I thought that a simple question wasn't important enough to share.

That was until one night when my cat knocked over a basket and out tumbled a crumpled orange note I had saved. In shaky handwriting it read: "I wish my teacher knew I don't have pencils at home to do my homework." As I reread those words, I felt the same ache as the first time I had read them. I thought of my former student, and how even though she didn't always have access to basic resources, she still came to school every day so willing to try, willing to struggle, and willing to learn.

After years of teaching, I have learned the sad reality is that her situation was far from unique. I wondered what the millions of children in our country's classrooms would say to their teachers if given the opportunity. I decided to share the activity with other teachers. I took a picture of the note with my cell phone and uploaded it to my new Twitter account. I typed in this girl's words and hit the Tweet button.

My goal in posting this little girl's note was to share a simple message with other educators: that students will share their realities with us if we simply give them an invitation. The real power of this exercise, and why so many people responded to it, has to do with the raw truth of the student's' words. When we are willing to really listen, our students might feel safe enough to express their truth. As teachers we need to ask, so that students will answer. But we also need to listen, so our students are heard.

Soon I began to get messages from around the world. I heard from teachers inspired to ask their students the same question and who began to share their responses. States away, fellow teachers had their students complete the simple sentence. Notes written on index cards began to form meaningful relationships between teachers and students.

Once the response on social media gained momentum, the news media took notice. A journalist from ABC News wrote a blog post and the idea took off from there. I was taken aback as news cameras rushed to our school. On one hand, I was surprised that humble handwritten notes could cause such a stir, but on the other hand, I think that the challenges our students face and the incredible work happening daily in our classrooms deserve attention.

It should make headline news that there are so many dedicated students who do not have pencils at home, but it doesn't. There should be outrage that many American children attend schools that lack necessary resources to teach them. We need to demand change. We must take action, both inside and outside the classroom, so that the American public education system is worthy of the brilliant students it serves. Harnessing the collective power of the voices of teachers, students, and their families is our best chance of creating the equitable system our country needs.

I believe in my students, and not just because that is what I'm supposed to do as a teacher. I hold a firm belief that my students will change the world. I warn each of them that if I don't get an invitation to their graduation, I will show up anyway. I am always telling my students, "The day I get to vote for one of you will be the happiest day of my life," and I mean it. I believe in my students because I know them. I see their potential, and I need that potential to be realized so that our city and our world become a better place.

Imagine a world in which every child's potential is valued; where every child receives the excellent education they deserve. What would our government look like? What would our neighborhoods look like? What would our schools look like? What would our classrooms look like? What would school be like if we asked students to tell us what we adults don't know?

What My Teachers Didn't Know

Growing up, I hated school. My students are always shocked to hear that their warm and cuddly teacher once felt like a bad apple and acted like a class bully. I hope sharing my experience shows my students that everyone can change and grow, like I did.

Especially in elementary school, I was *that* kid who was constantly in trouble. I remember one year, I had a teacher who wrote the names of kids in trouble on the whiteboard each day. I don't think she even bothered with the hassle of erasing my name because "Kyle S." was consistently on the board.

At that point in my life, I said exactly what I thought, at the exact moment I thought it. I never burdened myself with politeness or tact. I challenged anyone with authority. More than once I found myself inside the principal's office as my parents were informed of my bad behavior. I never imagined I would grow up and become my archnemesis: an elementary school teacher.

I did not always struggle in school. Until I was five years old, I grew up in Farmingdale, an unincorporated community in central Illinois not too far away from land worked by my family for over a century.

I attended kindergarten at a school surrounded on all sides by cornfields. Like so many of the families whose children I teach now, mine fell on hard times. Both of my parents were out of work and the unemployment money was running out. In the great American tradition, my father headed out West, searching for work. Eventually, my father found a job, rented an apartment, and sent for my mother, sister, and me to join him.

Our family landed right in the middle of Denver's preplanned suburban sprawl. Instead of corn tassels, beige roofs blanketed the landscape. I remember wondering why there were so many fences around yards if there were no cows inside. The shift from my small town to suburban life was difficult for me. On the first day at my new school, other students pointed out that I spoke with a country accent, and asked me why I wore strange clothes. Another student might have become withdrawn, but I met my classmates' curiosity with hostility.

While I had lovely teachers, none appreciated my inability to navigate this cultural shift. Looking back, I am surprised at the strategies I deployed to cope with this situation in such pragmatic and ultimately destructive ways. I shut down, put up my guard, and decided I didn't need to form relationships with anyone. I didn't need any new friends. I had friends back in Illinois. I even remember thinking, "I need to be mean to other kids before they have the chance to be mean to me," and I was only in first grade. As a nine-year-old, I kept a mental list of mean things to say to each of my classmates, just in case the need arose.

This was a miserable way to live, and it certainly made everyone around me miserable as well. I was hurtful to my peers, an annoyance to my teachers, and an overall challenge for my gentle, good-natured parents who struggled to manage such a strong-willed child. This feeling lasted well into adolescence and tainted my attitude toward education. I continued to be *that* kid. The student no teacher wanted on her class list, and what's worse—I knew it.

In my mind there were the "good" kids and the "bad" kids. I longed to be a *good* kid. The good kids always had nice clothes and combed hair, they said sweet things to the teachers, and they never forgot their backpacks on the kitchen table. It took my full concentration to not interrupt my teacher or blurt out a question, but it seemed like the good kids did not even have to try. They could sit attentively and politely, and most importantly the good kids knew how to be quiet. I resented how they effortlessly earned the approval of adults and the support of their peers.

I'm sure my teachers thought I did not care about school or making friends, but the truth was I stayed awake at night reliving every mistake of the day. I secretly listened to talk radio at night to distract my mind enough to sleep. I would sometimes have pep talks with myself. I would say, "Okay, today you are not going to make the teacher mad." Sometimes it worked, but inevitably I would lack the impulse control to keep quiet, or would snap at another student.

When a teacher reprimanded me, I refused to show emotion. Instead of crying, I drew miniature teardrops on the corners of my worksheets and pinched the skin on the inside of my wrist. To my teachers, I was a kid who did not care about anyone and was affected by nothing, but in reality the inner turmoil was eating me alive. Feeling like the bad kid was exhausting.

The cycle went on. I misbehaved, got in trouble, acted like I did not care, and secretly hated myself. Until middle school when we got real report cards for the first time. Opening up the thick orange envelope, I was shocked to see a line of straight As. Being the bad kid was ingrained in my identity, and good grades did not fit that image. I had a strange thought: "Maybe school is a place for me." Something began to change in me. My teachers still struggled with my behavior and challenging attitude, but I softened and began to develop friendships. I joined sports teams and was even elected to student government.

After doing the "I wish my teacher knew" exercise with my students, I began to reflect on my experience in school and how it could have been different. I am grateful for the teachers who put up with more than their fair share of attitude and still helped me learn.

What I realize now is that I never reached out to my teachers. I wish my teachers had known my bad behavior and bravado were a result feeling like I didn't belong. I wish my teachers had known I desperately wanted to please them, even though I appeared apathetic.

In retrospect, I am aware of all the benefits I had, even though I felt lost and angry growing up. I lived in a stable, supportive home. My parents provided me with all the resources I ever needed and all the love I could have ever asked for. I never worried about where my next meal would come from or how long I would be able to sleep in the same bed.

I did not have a learning disability. I was able to cling to my academic success to pull me out of my troubled behavior. My experience in school was different from many students. Struggles in reading never made me feel inadequate and math problems never made me feel defeated. My parents had been successful in school themselves, so they understood the concepts I was being taught and knew how to help me with my homework. I wonder what my life would look like if any of these factors had been different.

Perhaps if I had experienced any additional challenges or discrimination, I might have continued feeling irritated and isolated. I might have forever felt a lingering resentment toward the "good" kids. I might have thought of school as nothing more than a place where I disappointed and hurt people. If my family's financial situation had been different, I might have seen college tuition as an insurmountable obstacle. My education might have been sacrificed in order to find a place where I felt valued.

How many of the students that we teach have my story, but with a much different ending? How many of these students, with challenging circumstances, are slipping through the cracks?

My Path

I realized just how different my life could have been in 2008 when I moved to Washington, DC, to work with the education nonprofit City Year. As an AmeriCorps member I painted murals, scrubbed graffiti off school buildings, and served food to the homeless. I organized volunteer events that invited willing hands to build bookshelves for libraries and clean up city parks. In addition to those activities, I participated in a program called For Love of Children. I was partnered with an energetic kindergartener named Kaleb. He was bright, lively, and I absolutely adored him. Kaleb and I played word games and practiced writing his name in thick red marker. As the year went on, I realized what I really wanted to do was work toward giving kids like Kaleb a better opportunity to succeed in school.

After City Year, I completed college and moved to South America to work in schools in Chile. When I returned stateside, I headed back to my hometown of Denver. I knew that kids there deserved dedicated teachers, and hoped to become one.

I was accepted into the Denver Teacher Residency program. This program prepares teachers a little bit differently than conventional colleges and universities. I worked as a student teacher for an entire school year while also earning a master's degree in education. The most meaningful component was working side by side in the classroom with a distinguished teacher named Rachel Bernard. Each day, I observed rigorous instruction that supported learners at all levels, and had the opportunity to experience the cadence of a full school year firsthand.

This wasn't just a few weeks of student teaching; we planned and taught lessons together. I benefitted from constant, meaningful feedback from a trusted mentor, a luxury for a novice teacher. The feedback I received from her was not biased, toned down, or full of educational buzzwords. I learned so much that never appeared in any teaching textbooks.

For example, after I taught my first lesson, Ms. Bernard noted, "Next time, you need to address the four students in the corner who were having a sword fight with their pencils." Reflecting on my practice as an educator became second nature, but the most important lesson Ms. Bernard taught me was that "learning does not happen in a vacuum; you have to create a community."

During the school year a new student transferred into our class. The child had experienced deeply traumatic events and had a great deal of difficulty participating in classroom life. I was focused on the challenge that this new student presented. But Ms. Bernard told me, "Kyle, you have to find one thing you genuinely like about each student. Even if everything else is hard to manage, you have to hold on to at least one thing you appreciate. If kids think you don't like them, they will not learn from you."

Every day she took time to ask each student what was going on in their life. She celebrated their successes and consoled them when they were hurting. The community built in our classroom was strong. We knew each kid's favorite activities and what they wanted to be when they grew up. Our students that year worked hard and learned so much, but I did too. I learned that my students will carry the relationships created in our classroom with them.

Connection and Community in the Classroom

It's important to remember that the ability to build a connection with children, at any age, is not a fixed skill that some of us have and some of us do not. All educators can facilitate open communication, build strong relationships, and create a sense of community with the children they interact with. These objectives may not be written in curriculum manuals, but they are as essential to education as math and science.

In this book, I offer a perspective on how teachers can create a positive learning environment for every student, in every grade. In the chapters that follow, I provide a look at systemic issues like poverty and student mobility that affect millions of students nationwide, alongside problems that affect individual children and families, such as coping with trauma and creating friendships. In addition to statistics and research, I provide real stories from students, teachers, and family members that shed light on how we can all help students tackle these challenges and grow as individuals. I'll share strategies that have worked in classrooms across America as well as tips and techniques that have helped me create a community of third graders at Doull, year after year.

The ultimate goal of my work as a teacher (and as the author of this book) is to show my students how to become active and generous members of their communities, both inside and outside their classrooms. I believe I share that goal with you, and every educator in America. When we teach students the value of community, we show them how to live and grow among others, how to be generous and compassionate, how to be a good friend, how to help others feel appreciated, and how to contribute to our global community.

Fortunately, I find myself in good company, working among millions of strong, dedicated, and generous colleagues, and families who share the same mission. Join us in building a community within each classroom that not only creates academic success for children, but also helps create a generation of future adults who seek to welcome and encourage others, who are passionate lifelong learners, and whose experience in our classrooms made all the difference.

Every child deserves an excellent education. Every child deserves to feel cared about and heard. That starts by finding out what our students wish we knew.

wish my teacher knew that
she broke my heart when
she declared that my
art isn't good enough.

wish my teacher knew
that it's difficult to pay atten
in class, not knowing where I stay
going to sleep at night

wish my
teacher
knew I
re my
famil

I wish my teacher knew that
I've lived a hard life and I try
my hardest and best to remain
in the present of the day

I wish my teacher knew
that none of my friends from
my last school are like the people
I go to school with now.

wish my teacher knew
at my mom and
a argument ev
effect me a
hen they do
nes and my

knew th
to a diff

wish my teacher knew
at moving schools its
rel to make friends
th people you feel don't
e you.

knew
 my own aunt got diagnos
with cancer this week and I
been without a home 3 diff
times this year alone

I wish my teacher knew that
I hated to go back to the scho
y night & it was difficult to
pay attention in class

wish my teacher knew that
metimes my feelings and
tions are already crushed when I
valk into class and he/she
akes it worse by being hostil

I wish m
teacher
knew I

not provoke kids when they
ont even what's going on at
ome.

1.

Welcomes and Farewells
Building Community Even in Transition

My Classroom Community

"Ms. Schwartz, I have a big surprise for you," a gleeful voice called out. With thick coke-bottle glasses magnifying his brown eyes, Ronaldo took pride in being the first student to line up each morning when the bell rang. "I read for two hours last night," he told me, as he put his homework in the basket. Despite English being his second language, Ronaldo was reading a year above grade level. His dream was to be a scientist, and he was always ready to tell you a surprising fact about Venus or volcanoes.

Then one fall day, Ronaldo's life changed forever. He arrived at school and told me matter-of-factly that he wouldn't be in my third-grade class much longer. I was told that his father had been detained by the police. The family fought his deportation, but when news came that their appeal had been denied, Ronaldo's parents made the difficult decision to leave the life they had built in Denver, so that the family would not have to live divided between two countries.

To Ronaldo, the idea of moving to Mexico brought mixed emotions. Of course, being reunited with his father was welcome, but doing so at the cost of leaving the only life he had ever known was intimidating. From the information I had, Ronaldo had been born in the United States and was therefore a US citizen. Colorado was his home. He had attended our school since preschool and had formed tight friendships with his classmates; he was the darling of every teacher who had ever taught him.

Before leaving for Mexico, Ronaldo made his last days at our school count. He never missed a single homework assignment, even though an official grade would never be recorded. As the days ticked down, he took it upon himself to come to school each morning with an additional assignment completed: a letter carefully handwritten on blue-lined paper. His first was for me:

> Dear Ms. Schwartz,
> Thank you for all you have done to teach me, thank you for helping me learn. I will always remember you. Do not forget about me.
> Sincerely,
> Ronaldo

The next day he brought a letter for the principal. His former teachers, the school secretaries, even the lunch ladies all received farewell notes from Ronaldo. He penned letters to each of his friends, thoughtfully thanking them for their friendship and imploring each to remember him.

If my life had been uprooted, my father taken away, and I knew I would likely never see my friends or teachers again, my initial response certainly would have been a flood of anger and resentment. Likely Ronaldo experienced these same feelings, but he also made a deliberate choice to display gratitude. Watching him approach such a trying situation with maturity beyond his years taught me a powerful lesson about grace under pressure.

On his last day with our class, we took as many pictures as we could. Students presented their own letters to Ronaldo, recounting their memories, pledging their lasting friendship, and wishing him luck on his journey. There was some scuffling about who would sit next to him at his last lunch and who would get the privilege of playing with him during his final recess. The students signed pages of a book for him, and presented him with a plastic shark's tooth necklace so he could be "strong like a shark," which he showed off proudly for the rest of the day. As the bell rang on his final day with us, there were several students in tears due to their love for Ronaldo. An unspoken anxiety that a similar situation could arise for other families hung in the air.

"Don't forget me," Ronaldo implored me more than once before he left. He need not have worried. Ronaldo is the type of student that will forever be etched in a teacher's memory. If anything, I hope he remembers me. Such a child, brimming with potential and committed to learning, could certainly achieve great things.

I hope that wherever Ronaldo is, he is learning and happy.

America's Mobile Students

Like me, all teachers have seen students come and go from our classroom communities. When we look at these arrivals and departures nationally, they begin to tell a story of how common student mobility is in today's classrooms. We can also begin to understand the causes of student mobility and the implications these movements have on a student's education.

"Student mobility" is a term educators use to describe the phenomenon of students changing schools for any reason other than grade promotion. The widely cited, and still continuing, Early Childhood Longitudinal Study has followed a representative sample of kindergarten students since 1998 and found that by the time this cohort entered fifth grade, 61 percent of students had made at least one school change. Another wide-reaching analysis of student mobility led by Dr. Russell W. Rumberger of the University of California, Santa Barbara, found that 16 percent of fourth-grade students had moved schools more than twice in the last two years.

We now know that nearly all students will change schools before entering high school. A 2010 report by the Government Accountability Office (GAO) found significant differences between the 70 percent of students who are "less mobile" (who changed schools two times or less before entering high school) and the 13 percent of students who were "more mobile" (who changed schools four or more times). Researchers found that "students who changed schools four or more times were disproportionately poor, African American, and from families that did not own their home or have a father present in the household."

We also know that student mobility does not simply affect individual students. It affects school communities as a whole. In the United States, there are "high mobility" schools, termed this way because they serve a disproportionate share of those more mobile students. The GAO study found that 11.5 percent of all schools serve a student body that consists of more than 10 percent more-mobile students. It was also found that schools with high rates of student mobility also tend to serve more students who live in poverty, qualify for special education services, and are learning English; they also have higher absenteeism than schools with low mobility rates.

Students who are more mobile tend to go to schools where resources are already stretched thin in order to serve students with greater needs. This means that student mobility cannot be fully understood when looked at as a singular issue; it is interwoven with complex socioeconomic issues. In reality, mobility is just one symptom of many different factors that affect our students.

Why Are Our Students Mobile?

American students move for a multitude of reasons, but there are two basic categories each move can fit into: voluntary and involuntary. Voluntary moves obviously involve choice. A family might buy a new house and therefore change schools or consciously decide to make a school change. I changed elementary school every two years as a child, simply because the population in my suburb was growing so quickly that new schools were constantly being built to meet the demand.

The difference between a voluntary move and an involuntary move matters because as Rumberger explains, "Voluntary moves are often planned in advance, they often take place between school years to minimize the disruption to students' educational lives. In contrast, involuntary moves often occur during the school year and, hence, can be more disruptive to students' educational experience."

In my classroom, families have reported to me that they chose to enroll or unenroll their children in my school for a variety of voluntary reasons. One father told me the last school had assigned an overwhelming amount of homework. Other parents have pointed to a perception of disrespect from teachers at the former school. Another family simply wanted their elementary-aged children to attend school near their middle school–aged child. One of my students, Licia, left our school because her older brother was accepted to a nearby arts school and she was able to attend as well. Even though Licia knew in advance that she would be changing schools, it was a source of worry for her. She would tell me, "I know it's for my family, but I don't want to leave my best friends. I like it here."

Involuntary causes of student mobility vary as well. Sometimes these moves can be the result of a family change such as a death or a divorce. Economic factors play a role as well. Many families move when there has been a job loss or the cost of living has increased. Housing instability can play a major role in some communities. When I was student teaching, my colleagues who had taught at the school for a number of years noticed a trend also noted by the Government Accountability Office. It seemed some students were changing schools on a cycle. We realized that the apartments near the school ran a "one month free" special on rent. Families would pay the first month's rent, get the second month's rent free, not be able to pay the third month, and then be evicted.

A teacher I work with used to witness these evictions first-hand:

I worked in the legal department of a property management company for one year. Most of my responsibilities entailed filing legal documents to evict tenants who had become delinquent on their rent. One day, I worked with the local sheriff to evict a family. Hours passed as I watched them stack all of their possessions into lopsided piles on the sidewalk. I remember clearly the expression on each one of their faces. The children looked scared and confused, but it was their mother's distraught face that is burned into my memory. The family had nowhere to go. That day affected me profoundly. I was no longer willing to contribute to the desperation I saw that day. The next day I signed up for a teacher-training program. That family is the reason I teach today.

A student changing schools because of an eviction is an example of disruptive mobility. According to the National Center for Homeless Education, common causes of student mobility are poverty, migratory families, homelessness, immigration, and children being placed in foster care. And that's not all; an individual student might be dealing with several of these issues at the same time. When there is a sudden, involuntary change in schools for a student, there are almost always challenging circumstances surrounding it that teachers need to be aware of.

Ronaldo's story is just one of many. In 2013, the Center for Public Integrity shared records from the Applied Research Center demonstrating that "between July 2010 and September 2012, more than 105,000 people claiming to have US citizen children were deported." In my four years of teaching, there has always been at least one student in my classroom dealing with the deportation of a parent or a family member.

Likewise, I have consistently taught students who struggle with homelessness. My students have told me they slept in their car the night before, they had moved into an aunt's garage, or they were staying with another family until they could find a

I wish my teacher knew that my famly and I live in a shelter.

place of their own. Teachers may think all children who are homeless live in a shelter, but this is not true. Nearly three-quarters of homeless students live "doubled up," meaning they stay with friends or extended family members. Teachers might not even be aware that a student in their classroom is struggling with homelessness.

Sadly, the chances of having a student who is homeless in our classrooms rise every year. We now have more homeless students in our nation's schools than ever before. According to a US Department of Education report, homelessness is on the rise with school-aged children. During the 2012–13 school year, there were 1,258,182 homeless students in American public schools. Of students who are homeless, 16 percent are children with disabilities and 14 percent have not yet acquired English.

Each move our students make has a story attached to it. Our work is to listen to those stories. The more we know about the causes of mobility in our particular students, the better able we are to meet their needs and advocate for solutions that will provide support for our communities.

Military-Connected Students

Students are almost never in control of when and where they move. But for more than 2 million American students, their living situation is dictated by a powerful force: the US military. Students who are the official dependents of a military service member are known as military-connected students. The rates for mobility in military-connected students are triple that of their civilian peers. If a parent or caregiver is on active duty, typically there is a move every two to three years.

The Department of Defense operates 172 schools for military-connected students both within the United States and abroad. But 80 percent of military-connected students are educated in public schools by teachers who are often unaware of exactly who these students are. A great first step for teachers and school administrators is to identify these students with a simple conversation, or even as part of an initial questionnaire, so they can better meet these students' specific needs.

Sandra Temple (whose name has been changed in accordance with Department of Defense regulations) is a military-family life counselor serving students attending several schools on and near an American military base. Her role is to support students and families "struggling under the effects of extended and repeated deployments." She says, "Teachers should be prepared to help military-connected children and their families advocate for their educational needs. The truth is, 67 percent of children of active duty military families are under the age of twelve. These are typically children with younger parents who no longer live in their home communities and are disconnected from extended family. Under these circumstances, advocating for the needs of their children can be difficult, especially when entering a new school."

Temple also sees the impact of military mobility play itself out in students' behavior:

> Moving at the military's direction can be a major stressor for students. I often see students using coping strategies to lessen the pain of continuously leaving a community. Students begin to isolate themselves and detach from their friends and teachers, so it is easier to leave. A child might sabotage their friendships by engaging in bullying behavior or be reluctant to participate in group activities. Teachers can support students by acknowledging that what they are going through is tough. At one of the bases where I worked, several children found out which of their teachers had actually been raised as military kids themselves. They then asked those teachers for their advice on moving. The document those teachers created became a resource for the children. It helps them so much to know that they are not alone in facing their challenges. However, when you realize that only about one percent of the total US population is on active duty, you can understand why military children can feel so alone.

The School Superintendents Association recommends that schools make necessary exceptions for military-connected students when it comes to absences, registering for required classes, and transferring into the same grade level, regardless of age limits or district policy. Transferring credits and meeting changing graduation requirements are additional challenges facing these students. It is particularly important to address the needs of military-connected students who qualify for special education services. For teachers, obtaining a copy of the most recent Individualized Education Plan is essential to ensuring that each military-connected student's needs are met as soon as they enter school. Teachers can help advocate for their students by pointing to the Interstate Compact on Educational Opportunity for Military Children, which has been signed by every state, and helps address issues of "enrollment, placement, attendance, eligibility and graduation."

Teachers can also assist a student who is leaving by compiling resources to be given to the family and then passed on to the child's next teacher. Included should be relevant information about the student's academic progress and the content and curriculum that has been covered.

As Temple advises, "Military-connected students come from a unique and strong community. While they do need special consideration when entering or leaving your classrooms, there is also a wealth of experience and skills they bring that can be leveraged into meaningful learning when it is valued by a teacher."

Learning and the Mobile Student

Whether a student is connected to the military or not, the students in our classrooms who change schools often need additional attention. These moves have a sizable impact on their learning. While student mobility has been widely studied, its complicated nature makes it hard for researchers to make causal links between student mobility and academic outcomes. Each time a student transfers to a different school, the circumstances are unique. Often, there are typically multiple intertwined social, economic, and family issues. For example, if a child moved due to a divorce, it is difficult to determine to what degree his academics were affected by the change in his family dynamic and what role the move itself played.

In Dr. Russell W. Rumberger's analysis of several studies regarding student mobility, researchers found that mobility does have an impact on academic achievement, the strength of a student's friendship network, the likelihood of experiencing depression, and even the likelihood of being arrested. He explains there is evidence that "even one nonpromotional school move reduced both elementary school achievement in reading and math and increased high school dropout rates, with the most pronounced effects for students who made three or more moves." A 1996 study that analyzed students in Chicago Public Schools published by David Kerbow found that students who were highly mobile could be as much as four months behind their schoolmates by fourth grade. By sixth grade, these highly mobile students could be as much as a full year behind academically.

However, it is possible to limit the impact of changing schools. A different assessment of research published in 2008 shows that having social support from family and peers makes a big difference. More specific studies that examined the impact of the transition to middle school or high school indicate that support from peers and teachers positively influences the academic and social adjustment of adolescent students to a new environment.

In other words, we teachers can make a huge difference in the lives of students who are mobile. We can support our students with strategies that help them to feel welcomed and cared about.

Teacher Tools

1. Start with the Relationship

The first few days of any school year are all about getting to know our students as people and setting firm expectations for what the coming year will bring. When a new student enters our classrooms in the middle of the year, they have missed out on all that community-building work, and teachers need to make up for lost time by ensuring our first words to a new student count.

The second a new student enters a new classroom, our primary focus should be on building a relationship. Being the new kid at school is a high-stress situation, no matter how old a student is. By simply saying something like "I'm glad you are here," right away you and the new student have a great start. Letting a student know you are happy they are in your class can allow for a sigh of relief and make nervous shoulders drop four inches. Find several opportunities during the day to reinforce the idea that the new student is appreciated and welcomed. Be relentless.

After introducing yourself and welcoming a new student to class, the next thing you should say is "Sit here." Directing a student to their seat may seem obvious or even innocuous, but it is necessary. Classrooms often have a secret code of who sits where that can be difficult for new students to navigate. Saying "Find a seat anywhere" will likely make a student feel nervous, out of place, even terrified to make a mistake.

Finally, the last step to solidifying a new student's place in your classroom community is asking the student to contribute. I have found much success in my classroom by asking new students to help in some small way. Make sure, however, that you *ask* for help rather than command a new student to do a task. "Can I ask you for a favor? Would you mind pushing in the chairs for me? I really need some help" will have a much different impact than "Push in those chairs." The task could be as simple as turning off the lights, putting away markers, or erasing the board. It's hard for even the most angst-ridden teenagers to refuse help to someone they just met when they are asked politely. Every student I have ever taught has found so much joy in being helpful.

After the new student completes the task, make sure to show your gratitude. Focus your praise on how the student has made a contribution to the community. You might say, "Thank goodness you're here, we need someone kind like you in our class to help hold the door for us." Or, "It's so great that you're tall. We needed someone to reach that cabinet." It might seem simple, but by asking a new student to do something helpful you will transform a child from someone waiting to see if they are accepted by a new group into a contributing member of a classroom community. Students, especially those who have moved a lot, want to feel they are needed and genuinely welcomed into a classroom community, not just assigned to a class.

I saw this happen firsthand on Benji's first day of school. He was simply dropped off at the front of the building. No one walked him into the office or told him where to go. A helpful student asked him if he was lost and showed him to our classroom. Entering a new school in the middle of the year must have been difficult for him; rules and relationships had already been established. I am sure it made walking into a new school even more challenging that there was no one there to shepherd him in. If it had been me, I would have felt intimidated and certainly not welcomed.

So I followed my simple steps. I made it very clear to Benji that he was welcome and that our class was excited to have a new student. I got him set up in a seat right away and gave him a manageable task: to decorate his own name tag. Once this was underway, I praised him. "Those are great colors, how did you choose them?" I asked. Benji told me they were the colors of his favorite football team. Then I asked him if he would use his artistic abilities to make a sign for our classroom door with our room number. He gladly obliged and started decorating a big "Room 207" sign. Other students chimed in with compliments on his art skills as I sent him out to the hall with a few new friends to hang up the sign. Within fifteen minutes, Benji transformed from a lost little boy to a contributing member of the community, who had already begun to form relationships with his classmates.

When another new student, Sigrid, entered our classroom, I again focused on building the relationship. When she arrived at our door, she was hiding behind her mother, who had clearly prepared for this day. She had slicked her daughter's shiny auburn hair into two perfect pigtails and dressed her in a bright outfit.

Sigrid looked beyond me to the seeming chaos of students setting up chairs and turning in homework. I saw her trying to hold back tears, which ultimately started trickling down her face. She began sobbing. What do you do when a child you just met is crying uncontrollably?

I got down on Sigrid's level and looked her right in the eye and said, "I know this is hard." I quickly told her I had had been the new kid in elementary school four times, and each time I worried about making friends. I let her know our class was a wonderful class, we had nice kids, and we had awesome books to read. I told her our class was lucky to have her and that we needed her there. Then I showed her to the water fountain and told her we had a seat waiting for her when she was ready.

Later in the year, the students wrote a paragraph explaining a time when they felt sad. Part of Sigrid's paragraph read, "I was sad on my first day of school, but then Ms. Schwartz told me she

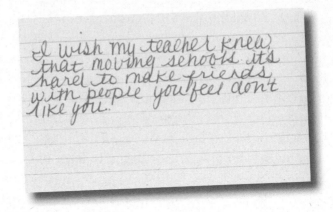

I wish my teacher knew that moving schools its hard to make friends with people you feel don't like you.

was the new kid once and it made me feel better so I stopped crying."

Children need comfort and reassurance. They also need touchstones in a strange environment, but most of all they need a teacher willing to build a relationship with them from the very beginning.

2. Welcome Kits

A few months into my first year of teaching, our school secretary stopped me on the way into school. She told me a new student, Mirrana, would join our class that day. She also told me this new student used a wheelchair. This was the first time I had ever been assigned a new student. I frantically ran up to my room to arrange the tables in my classroom so Mirrana could access our room. I had to track down our custodian to see if he could raise a table so her wheelchair could fit underneath it. All of a sudden, the bell rang. Nothing was ready and I was flustered.

Looking back, I think of how Mirrana must have felt as she entered my classroom. I was concerned about the logistics of adding a new student, but she was concerned about feeling welcome. As the year went on, I was able to build a meaningful relationship with her, but I'm sure the transition could have gone more smoothly.

Ever since then, I have made it a point to have the essentials ready for a new student in a welcome package. New students experience so much trepidation about their first day. They are anxious about being singled out and worried about making a connection with their peers and teachers. The last thing they need is an overwhelmed, unprepared teacher.

Generally, I expect about five new students to enter my classroom at some point in the year. So I create Welcome Kits. It does not take much extra time or effort because I do this as I am setting up my classroom at the beginning of the year. As I prepare for the first day of school, I set aside extra materials for potential new students.

I fill five cardboard magazine boxes; each contains a homework folder, writing notebook, and name plate for the desk. I also include copies of welcome letters from back-to-school nights and important handouts. For older students, a teacher might include a class syllabus, a binder, and contact information. As a school, we are also able to give each student who enters in the middle of the year a pencil bag with basic school supplies such as pencils, markers, and glue sticks donated from Yoobi, a philanthropy-focused school supply company. It is a very practical and tangible way to make new students feel welcome and cared about.

Molly Couture, the office manager at the Denver School of Science and Technology, takes the Welcome Kit a bit further.

Our school has a strong onboarding process for new students at the beginning of the school year, but I realized that some students were falling through the cracks when they transferred to our school in the middle of the school year. One year, on the very last day of school, a student told me shyly that no one had ever assigned him a locker. I knew we needed to get systematic so that nothing gets skipped. Our office created a Welcome Passport for students registering in the middle of the year. Students now go through a comprehensive checklist that makes sure all their administrative needs are met. This also serves to teach new students about the culture of our school and introduce them to the teachers and staff members that can support them when needed. For me, it is important to ensure our school is prepared make new students feel welcomed right away.

I also see an opportunity to get our current students and families involved in the creation of Welcome Kits. A student council could be put in charge of creating them the kits. As students, they might have a better idea of what items would be helpful to include. Perhaps giving a new student an extra school shirt or free tickets to school dances and sports events would encourage them to join in.

This idea could even be expanded to include the whole family. Welcome Kits can be adapted to meet the needs of local communities. Imagine giving a new family a backpack full of books or a packet of coupons to local restaurants. One school might include winter hats and gloves. Another might include coins for a local Laundromat, or subway cards. Having the school community give thought to the needs of students who will inevitably enter their school in the middle of the year helps create a welcoming culture.

Welcome Kits have helped me do just that. Since I have already put thought into how I am going to welcome a new student, even when I am given no warning, these premade Welcome Kits make students feel they already have a place in our community. I feel prepared to welcome a student at any time.

3. Making Hellos and Farewells Official

When a student joins my class in the middle of the year, it is often due to a major change in their life. A few words of encouragement from their teacher can make a student feel valued. Sending home a simple handwritten note with a new student can be powerful. A letter might look like this:

> Hello Johana,
> I just wanted to tell you how excited I am that you are in our class. Thanks for telling me about your pet cat. Did you know our class is going to a baseball game next month? Do you like baseball?
> See you tomorrow,
> Ms. Schwartz
> P.S. Write me back!

You can take the idea of a welcoming letter to the next level by having your whole class sign it. A tangible note that tells a new student their teacher and class are happy to meet them and share a community together can be a powerful way to build a relationship.

These official notes can be especially meaningful to students of diverse cultures. When I was studying in China as a member of a Fulbright-Hays group, I noticed several times how

In My Classroom
Julian Roldan, Third-Grade Teacher

My whole life pivots on what happened to my family when I was twelve years old. I was born in San Juan, Puerto Rico. After our home was robbed several times in succession, my father announced we would be moving to the United States for better opportunities.

I was thrilled. I had gone to Disney World before, so naturally I thought America would be one big amusement park full of hotdogs and roller coasters. That was not the case when my family arrived in Denver, Colorado. I remember wondering why everything was so brown. My nose and throat felt full of sand in the arid climate. I remember my first day in an American school clearly. I felt awkward and self-conscious, but most of all I felt lonely.

My teacher was warm and welcoming. She took the time during her lunch breaks to pull me aside and ask me how I was doing. It was an opportunity for me to ask questions like what kind of clothes I should wear, how lunch and recess worked, and she laughed as she explained that the students were not pouring white paint on their food, it was actually a peculiar condiment called ranch dressing.

meaningful official documents were to Chinese students. Letters and awards were proudly displayed in homes and schools. One Chinese professor stopped his lecture to pull out an official thank-you note he had received and passed it around. This experience made me realize how to some people "officialness" is

In an effort to make me feel more included, my teacher asked me to stand up in front of the class and share a story about my life in Puerto Rico. I know she had the best intentions at heart, but all this did was embarrass me. I felt as if she singled me out just as I was trying so desperately to fit in. Looking back, I would have loved to share stories about my life with my classmates. I would have told them how much I missed the Cream of Wheat my abuela topped with brown sugar on lazy Sunday mornings. I wished the other kids shared their experiences with me too. I was just as curious about my classmates' lives as they must have been about mine.

As a teacher now I make a point of sharing my personal stories as a way of connecting and building relationships with my students. It is encouraging for my students to know that once upon a time their teacher was just like them. I too had the same butterflies in my stomach and felt the same concerns new students feel when coming into a new place. It's powerful for students to know that their teacher was once in their shoes.

Like my teacher years ago, I make sure to check in with new students so they know I care and am there to support them. My hope is that my students can feel their classroom is a safe space for sharing their unique background stories and experiences.

a prized gesture. So, if sending home an official letter helps a family feel welcome and valued, I'm all for it.

Once I even created an official Welcome Award. At our school, we have two awards ceremonies at the end of each semester. Teachers give out various certificates like art awards and honor roll awards. That year we were faced with a problem. Two students enrolled in our school a few days before the ceremony. Instead of having them sit idle and watch as their peers were cheered for while they received certificates, we whipped up two official Welcome Awards. The new students beamed as their names were called. Both students were able to take home an official award for their family to display on their refrigerator. It was such a success that our school is working on getting Welcome Awards to all new students. Schools might also consider hosting a welcome lunch each month to extend an official welcome.

Teachers and schools need to have plans in place to support students when they enter our communities, but we also need to give consideration to when students must go. When a student leaves a classroom community, often the teacher's immediate response is to remove all their things, take their names off the wall, and make space for the next student. I urge teachers not to do this. Don't erase students from your classroom community's collective memory. Instead, leave their name tags and work on the wall when possible. When students in my class asked why I still had Ronaldo's name tag up, I said, "Because I miss him and I like remembering all the fun times we had together in class. I want us all to remember him." It sends a message to the students who stay that everyone is a valuable member of the community.

When a student has to leave our class, I like to send them off with a stack of letters from the class. If our class knows in advance that a student is moving, I send a blank sheet of notebook paper home with simple instructions: "Write a letter saying goodbye to Ronaldo." The next day I always get back a stack of letters full of kind words and encouragement.

Students in my classroom are missed even when they move without warning. Like when one of my students, Jennilyn,

suddenly left. She was an enthusiastic learner, once announc-
ing to me, "Ms. Schwartz, I am going to remind you every day
that I am going to college." After Jennilyn had not shown up
for school for several days, our school secretary found out she
had just registered to attend another school in a different city.
Just like it must have been for Jennilyn, the sudden move was
difficult for the students in our class. They missed their friend
and didn't even have a chance to say goodbye.

To respond to this situation, I remembered advice from a
fellow teacher, Susana Moening. She told me that whenever
a student moved away her class wrote goodbye letters, even
when the move was unexpected and the student had already
left. Whenever she could, Susana delivered the letters to the
student's new school or home. If she couldn't locate where the
student had moved, she kept the letters waiting in a shoebox in
the classroom, just in case he or she ever returned. "Kids need
closure when relationships end. It is a teacher's job to take care
of the community," she told me.

I used this strategy as a way for our classroom community to
say goodbye to Jennilyn. The day we found out she had transferred schools, we all took a few minutes at the beginning of
class and wrote her letters. I was touched to read how much
kindness and empathy my students displayed in their writing.
I quickly compiled them and our school secretary sent them to
Jennilyn's new school along with her academic records.

This gave the class a sense of closure and reassured students
that if they ever moved away they would be missed. I like to
think of Jennilyn, sitting in her new classroom miles away,
suddenly receiving a big stack of letters and reading the warm
wishes and messages of encouragement from her friends. It's
nice to think that even though she was no longer with our class,
she still felt cared about.

4. Transition Mementos

Another way to show a child that they will be missed is to give them a Transition Memento. When a child is dealing with something out of their control, like moving and switching schools, sometimes it helps to give them something they can actually hold on to. Our classroom started a tradition to help students when they were leaving our classroom in the middle of the year.

When Ronaldo left, we gave him a shark's tooth necklace so that he could be "strong like a shark." I have seen other teachers print out a photograph of the class for classmates to sign.

There are no rules on what will make a good Transition Memento. It just needs to be meaningful to the class and student who is transitioning. You could give the student a rock from the playground or press some leaves from a tree. A favorite book or stuffed animal will work as well. With older students, creating a Transition Memento could be as simple as taking a class picture.

Whatever you choose as a Transition Memento, the departing student will feel cared about and appreciated. Students who leave your community will have something to hold in their hands as a reminder that there are people who care about them and miss them. This is yet another way to provide a sense of closure for the rest of your students because as their friend leaves, a piece of their classroom community will be carried away with them.

When a student comes or goes in our classrooms, we must remember that the individual student is not the only one in transition. As a new student arrives, we must model and expect welcoming behavior from the other members of the classroom.

It is equally important to consider how to make the class feel whole when a friend and classmate has to leave.

If national trends continue, more and more students will switch schools, and the effects are real.

As teachers we must investigate and understand the underlying causes of student mobility both nationally and in our communities. Issues like housing security and job security, though political in nature, play themselves out in our classrooms every day. They affect our students' ability to stay in our schools and learn. Educators can be the ones to elevate our students' stories and advocate for their needs.

Teachers need to deliberately prepare for the effects of student mobility in their classrooms. Each child who enters or leaves your classroom community has a story. It's up to us to support our students and ensure that transitioning into or out of our classrooms is a positive experience. As teachers, we can't always control when and why a student transitions to or from our school, but we can focus on what we do control: how we handle each situation. By having strategies ready, we can make students feel welcome and included when they arrive as well as valued and missed if they must leave.

wish my teacher knew that
she broke my heart when
she declared that my
art isn't good enough.

wish my teacher knew
that it was difficult to pay attention
in class, not knowing where I was
going to stay at night.

WISH MY
eacher
knew I
ve my
family

I wish my teacher knew that
I've lived a hard life and I try
my hardest and best to remain
positive even _____ of the day

wish my
ut my mom ____
a argument ____
effect me ____
hen they do
_____ and my

I wish that my teacher
knew that i struggle to get
to school (No transportation)
- I wish my teacher's
knew that i barely have time
to do my homework.

_____ knew th
____ to a chat

wish my teacher knew
at moving schools its
ard to make friends
th people you feel don't
e you.

_____ knew
my mom ____ get dangerous
with cancer this week and I
been without a home 3 diff
times this year alone.

I wish my teacher knew that
I hated to go back to the ____
y night & it was difficult to
attention in class

wish my teacher knew that
metimes my feelings and
otions are already crushed when
walk into class and he/she
akes it worse by being hostil

I WISH m
teacher
knew I

o not preceive kids when they
n't know whats going on at
me.

2.

Students and Poverty
Building on Resources and Breaking Down Barriers

My Classroom Community

The first year of teaching is such a trying experience for educators. But ask any of us and we all remember that first group of students with a particular glimmer in our eyes. As I tried to figure out exactly what kind of teacher I would be, I found my thoughts constantly pulled to what I could do to help each of my students pursue their interests and dreams.

One of my students, Chris, was obsessed with all things science. He even introduced himself as, "Hi, I'm Chris, I am going to be a scientist." Chris's bespectacled grin would greet me each morning accompanied by an explanation of a homemade experiment or a fact about dinosaurs. While most of my students' eyes willed the hands of the clock to move faster in anticipation of recess, Chris's nose was firmly placed betwixt the pages of a book.

As summer approached, I thought of ways Chris could explore his scientific interests, and I had just the right idea. I would find him a scholarship to a summer science camp. With just a few short emails, I secured him a spot in a science-focused summer camp, completely free of charge. I was thrilled.

I triumphantly announced the news to Chris and his mother after school one day. His eyeballs popped way open and his mouth dropped. "You mean I will get to meet real scientists?" Chris's mother was equally appreciative; her son's education was the highest priority. Anything she could do, she would do.

After I sent her the details about the summer camp. Chris's mother called me. She remorsefully explained that Chris would not be attending the science camp. With both parents working all day, it was impossible to drive her son to the camp in the morning and pick him up in the afternoon. It was something I hadn't even considered, likely because that would never have been a concern for me as a child. My parents could go into work late or leave early if it was necessary to drive me somewhere.

I had only good intentions when I found the science camp, but I was ignorant of the realities Chris faced. Like most students I have taught, Chris was understanding of his parents' situation, but of course he was discouraged. My insensitivity caused an uncomfortable situation. Chris and his parents were disheartened that he couldn't go to the science camp, and I felt responsible for their disappointment.

My false assumption that Chris's family had the resources to transport him every day to science camp was something I definitely had to learn from. I now know that, as a teacher, I need to work in partnership with my students' families. I learned early on in my teaching career that my blind spots have the potential to cause big problems, even when I have only the best of intentions.

Half of Our Students

Discussing the effects of poverty on students could fill several books, and has. As educators and community members, we need to understand the realities of poverty and its effects in American schools.

The numbers are staggering.

In 2011, 23,544,479 children attending public schools were living in households that met the federal requirements for the National School Lunch Program, an indicator of poverty according to the National Center for Educational Statistics. Statistics from 2013 cited by the *New York Times* indicate that an even higher number, roughly 51 percent, of all the children who walk into our public schools each morning live in poverty.

With over half of our students living in poverty, it is impossible for teachers to ignore how socioeconomic issues directly impact the learning in our classrooms. Nor is it possible to absolve ourselves of the responsibility of addressing it. Poverty is a complex issue, but teachers cannot leave the work of addressing it to others, because poverty issues are learning issues. Discussions on how to support our students need to take place at every level, from the White House to the street corner and, yes, in the teachers' lounge as well.

We have a responsibility as teachers to address issues of poverty in order to be truly effective educators. Part of this responsibility is to develop an understanding of the effects of poverty on our students' physical and emotional health as well as their academic achievement. It is clear that we cannot be effective educators if we do not understand the implications that living in poverty have on a student's school experience. We cannot develop and maintain authentic, genuine relationships with our students if we do not understand how poverty is affecting their lives both inside and outside our classrooms.

In my own journey to become an effective third-grade teacher, it is not enough for me to have content knowledge and well-developed instructional methods. If my students are to meet every inch of their academic potential, I must understand the barriers to education that exist for them. Otherwise, I run the risk of teaching with unchecked biases. I am proud to say that I work in a school building where so many others have dedicated themselves to the same pursuit.

On the most basic level, living in poverty means the basic needs of a child—love and affection, stable living conditions, proper nutrition, adequate health care, and a good learning environment—are not always being met. Poverty impacts a student's ability to receive the quality education they deserve, and yet a quality education can lift a student and an entire community out of poverty. This messy, symbiotic relationship between education and poverty is what we educators need to examine.

Poverty, Lunch, and the Minimum Wage

Among the most basic needs of a child is nutrition. We know that children who live in poverty struggle to get adequate quality food. Because of this, the federal government has stepped in to offer this most basic guarantee: that children living in poverty who attend school will be fed. The decision to feed our hungry students has altered the way policymakers measure poverty and changed the way educators talk about poverty.

If education is your field, you have heard the term "FRL." I hear conversations with phrases like "We are 98 FRL" and "Our

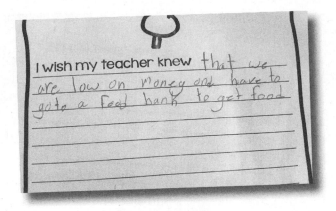

I wish my teacher knew that we are low on money and have to go to a food bank to get food

school went from 60 FRL to 76 FRL last year." Educators use these coded sentences as shorthand to describe how much a particular school is impacted by poverty.

FRL means "free or reduced-priced lunch." So how did lunch become a proxy for socioeconomic status? It all stems from a federal meal-assistance program called the National School Lunch Program, which addresses the clear link between poverty, food insecurity, and learning. As reported by Children's Healthwatch, "By kindergarten, food-insecure children often are cognitively, emotionally and physically behind their food-secure peers."

Sometimes we hear students who qualify for FRL or who live in poverty referred to as "low income," "underresourced," or "economically disadvantaged." These euphemisms serve to shield us from the reality that so many students in our country face dramatic challenges. I argue that we need to confront the brutal truth. When our government must step in and provide meals for students, it means those students are living in poverty. We can change the wording, but the reality remains the same.

In My Classroom

Valerie Wintler, School Nurse

My school, Kunsmiller Creative Arts Academy, is unique because our school educates students from kindergarten all the way through the twelfth grade. This allows me, as the school nurse, to watch kids grow up. It also means I am witness to how poverty manifests itself throughout a child's life. Poverty affects our students' learning in very real ways. One of the most observable effects of poverty is hunger.

Before we started a breakfast program, each day three or four elementary school students would show up in my health office in the midmorning complaining of headaches or stomachaches. Young students have a harder time identifying that the discomfort they are feeling is directly related to being hungry. But, as a nurse, I realized very quickly that these were not symptoms of an illness. In actuality they were the symptoms of hunger. It was causing students to miss out on learning time in their classrooms.

My older students are just as affected by hunger. However, years of living with food insecurity have taught them to disguise their symptoms better. Adolescent students who are experiencing hunger act irritably, feel dizzy, or have trouble focusing—all of which could easily be confused for behavior problems. My high school students do not want their peers to know they are struggling with hunger or that they do not have sufficient access to food. I have heard teens say they just do not want to eat or they just don't like the cafeteria food rather than admit they simply do not have the money to pay for it.

Many families at our school meet the requirements to qualify for free or reduced-price lunch, but there are still obstacles in their way. Sometimes families do not even realize that the school lunch program is available, but other times the paperwork alone is the challenge. That was the case for Brandon.

He was a common fixture in the principal's office as a result of misbehavior. One day, Brandon was sent to the office after punching a locker in a moment of frustration. While I treated the wounds on his knuckles, I asked him what he had eaten that day. He answered, "Nothing."

As I found out, most days he wasn't eating breakfast or lunch because he didn't have the money. The fixed income his grandmother, who was raising him, received would have qualified Brandon to receive free lunch, but for many reasons the forms were never filled out. Of course now that I know Brandon does not have stable access to food I make sure that he is fed. I am aware this does not address the root causes of his problem. And, regrettably, I know that American schools are filled with students who have the same story.

When it comes to school nursing, many people think the job entails Band-Aids and ice packs, but that is just scratching the surface. Our job is identifying and addressing health issues that can affect a student's learning. My role as a school nurse is to make sure that the students in our school are healthy enough to learn, and many times that means combating childhood hunger. That is why I am a strong advocate for my students. I cannot stand by and watch our students go hungry.

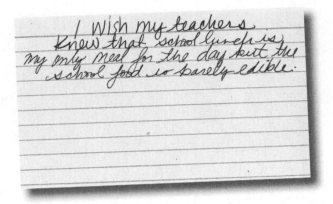

I wish my teachers knew that school lunch is my only meal for the day but the school food is barely edible.

In 1946, a growing understanding of the relationship between nutrition and learning prompted President Harry S. Truman to create one of the largest feeding programs in the history of our country and, importantly, he housed it inside our schools. Since its creation, more than 224 billion meals have been served to children inside the walls of our schools.

While educators frequently talk about free lunches, few understand the requirements. In order to qualify for free meals and milk through this program, students must live in households earning no more than 30 percent above the national poverty threshold. This threshold is determined by the federal government each year and does not take into account geographical differences in cost of living, as it is the same for the entire continental United States, although curiously Alaska and Hawaii have a different, higher threshold.

The eligibility requirements tell us about the income of our students' families. For the 2013–14 school year, this meant that a household of two, say a single parent and child, would qualify for free meals and milk if the family earned no more than $399 each week, or $20,748 before deductions annually. When the child attended school, he would receive free lunches, and his enrollment would count toward that school's FRL rate.

Let's use an example of a single parent with one child to investigate how this works. In a standard workweek this single parent would earn an hourly wage of $9.97, which is far above our federal minimum wage of $7.25 an hour. With some exceptions, if you work for minimum wage, your children qualify for free or reduced-price lunches. It could be said that the National School Lunch Program is subsidizing employers who pay the minimum wage by feeding their employees' children.

As evidenced by the existence of our National School Lunch Program, the federal government recognizes that students need proper nutrition to learn. But when we dig into the numbers, the program also acknowledges that the minimum wage is not a sufficient wage with which to feed a child. From the private sector to local governments, there is an abundance of opinions on what the ideal minimum wage should be. But seldom is the perspective of an educator solicited or considered.

Why should teachers care about the eligibility requirements for the National School Lunch Program and the minimum wage? Because it matters to our students. The minimum wage is a learning issue because it is arguably not a living wage. Half of our students are living in environments with food insecurity. Our school lunch program provides some meals to hungry students, but only on school days. It is not enough to ameliorate the effects of food insecurity on our students' learning.

Food insecurity is defined by the United States Department of Agriculture (USDA) as "consistent access to adequate food is limited by a lack of money and other resources at times during the year." Living in poverty, and therefore, living without consistent access to nutrition, affects a child's academic

What My Teacher Doesn't Know
Briti's Story

Many things in my life changed for my family when my mother courageously took legal measures to protect myself and my sisters from my father's abuse. When my father subsequently abandoned our family, suddenly there was no income in our home. The fear of living with an abusive father was quickly replaced by the stress and anxiety of financial uncertainty. Each member of my family had their role to play in keeping us afloat and it was now my shared responsibility to support us financially; all while trying to pass my sophomore year of high school.

Immediately, living in poverty caused me to live under a new burden of secrecy. Struggling financially was not the norm at my large suburban high school. I was not the only one in this same situation. There were several other students who felt isolated in an environment which seemed to be set up to serve the students who had easy access to money and resources. It felt like there was an overwhelming assumption that poor students just did not exist.

So I learned to hide my family's struggles. I intentionally went through the lunch line last so that no other students would see the register flash $0.00 and make the connection that I received free lunch. I dropped out of extracurricular activities to spare myself from having to ask for help paying the fees. Each day, I told my algebra teacher that I couldn't find my calculator instead of admitting that there was no money to purchase one. She never inquired further.

Poverty also led to my identity as a student being redefined. After being held in high esteem by my teachers as a dedicated and responsible student for my entire educational career, I was quickly made to feel as though I was insufficient and also a burden. I could feel their disappointment in me every time I did not have the required school supplies or failed to turn in assignments on time. It was remarkably easy for some teachers to assume that I was lazy and apathetic. But the truth was that I was working at a pizza place every night until midnight in a desperate effort to save my family's home from foreclosure.

During this time in my life, school was still my top priority. I felt a tremendous personal responsibility to pull myself and my family out of poverty. I knew the only way this could be done was by completing my education. At times, my schoolwork was compromised in an attempt to meet the immediate needs of my family. There were times when I had to make a difficult choice to skip math homework in order to pick up an extra shift at work, which would keep a roof over my family's head for one more month.

A few teachers and school counselors took the time to investigate what was really going on in my life. The empathy and understanding some teachers showed me during this time made me work harder to do well in their classes. I want teachers to know that students who are living in poverty value their education just as much if not more than other students, but we need their support and compassion.

success because, as a study published in the American Society for Nutritional Sciences concluded, "Food insecurity acts as a psychological or emotional stressor, affecting parent and child behavior."

The rate of the minimum wage and the amount of income in our students' homes affect their ability to eat and grow, and therefore to learn. Teachers need to understand how issues like food insecurity connect to the minimum wage and impact our classrooms, so that we can advocate for our students and teach them to become strong advocates from themselves.

Two Americas

Looking at how our nation's schools rank internationally tells a powerful story of how poverty affects our students' educational achievement. Administered every three years to fifteen-year-olds from member countries, the Programme for International Student Assessment (PISA) is an assessment that uses student scores to compare the world's educational systems.

America's ranking is clearly a cause for national embarrassment.

In the most recent data from 2012, our country ranked seventeenth in the world in reading and twenty-seventh in mathematics. The results of this exam tell a global story, but they also help illustrate what is really happening in our schools on a national level. When we look closely at the data, we see a story of two Americas: one with highly effective schools for the children of wealthy Americans, and one where schools are failing to meet the educational needs of students living in poverty.

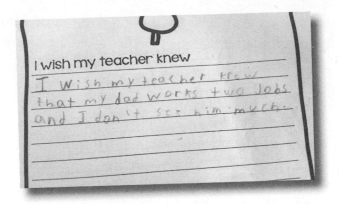

I wish my teacher knew

I wish my teacher knew that my dad works two jobs and I don't see him much.

The National Association of Secondary School Principals extrapolated the results of the PISA exam based on each school's concentration of poverty; that is, what percentage of students were living in poverty. Schools that had a low rate of poverty—10 percent or less—have the second to highest scores in the world. But at the same time, as reported by *NEA Today,* "In schools where 75 percent or more of the students get free or reduced lunch, the reading score was 446. That's off the bottom of the charts, below . . . Greece's 483." Simply put, the United States has both the best and worst schools in the developed world.

Apart from infuriating me with such clear inequity, the results of the PISA reveal another truth. In America, we know how to educate children. We are among the best in the world at it. We have the capacity and resources to lead the children who arrive in our schools as five-year-olds, and thirteen years later invite them to enter our society as the best-educated adults in the world. This ability is the source of our greatness.

However, the stark reality is that so many of our schools fail year after year to offer an effective and equitable level of education to children living in poverty. We can do better to educate all of our students, and need to start in our classrooms.

Teacher Tools

1. Resources and Barriers Chart

The vast majority of the students at my school live in poverty. Most have basic needs that are not being met, which leads to significant obstacles to academic success. But we limit the power of a school when the negatives are all we see. Too often our students, especially students living in poverty, come to school with resources we take for granted.

As educators, when we start recognizing things like joy, energy, and curiosity as resources and usable skills, we can leverage them in our classrooms. This is not just a fluffy teacher way of thinking. It's real. Think about how much energy and money adults spend trying to get a taste of the joy a kindergarten student experiences simply by rolling down a hill.

Acknowledging that these attributes are real and valuable is one way to help honor the resources students come to school with. The book *Building Communities from the Inside Out,* by John P. Kretzmann and John L. McKnight, presents the theory that effective community development efforts are based on understanding and utilizing the community's assets, capacities, and abilities. Kretzmann and McKnight comment, "The unique energy and creativity of youth is often denied to the community because the young people of the neighborhood are all too often viewed only in terms of their lack of maturity and practical life experience."

I wish my teacher knew that
that I hated to go back to the shelter
every night & it was difficult to
pay attention in class

Honoring all the resources our students bring, including their own disposition, strength of character, ambition, and enthusiasm, can help every student feel like an integral part of their classroom community. We can then mobilize and connect the resources our communities have in order to improve the community as a whole.

I witnessed my students' ability to inspire and provoke a conversation about realities in our education system through their simple "I wish my teacher knew" notes. Their words, not mine, reached all corners of the globe, proving that even eight-year-olds possess tremendous reserves of honesty and insight that can make a measurable impact.

Most teachers I know think in terms of strengths and needs. We ask, "What strengths does she have in math?" and "What is his greatest need in reading?" It is important to know the skills a student already possesses and, on the flip side, the academic gaps a student displays. We need to know where students need support. This type of analysis is certainly useful and necessary, but it is also helpful to think in terms of the resources and barriers that exist. This can be as simple as creating a "T-chart," and can be done for an individual student, a group of students, or a whole community. A chart might look like this:

Student: Mateo

Resources	Barriers
Athletic, loves to move physically	Often comes to school hungry
Speaks Spanish at home	Struggles with time management and turning homework in consistently
Dislikes when things seem to be unfair	Difficulty maintaining attention for more than ten minutes in a whole group lesson
Talks about what he saw on the news	
Father, mother and siblings attend his football games	Attempted to solve problems through physical fighting

As you can see in this example, thinking creatively in terms of what constitutes a resource can help us see the wealth students already possess. All students bring positive traits and skills to the classroom. Students who live in poverty are no different.

The student in the above analysis might complain when things are "unfair." A teacher can use this natural instinct to motivate him academically by focusing on studying powerful leaders who stood up when things were unfair, or by helping explore social issues that matter to him.

In my class we did just that. During a unit on biographies, my students realized there were no holidays that celebrated women. "That's not fair!" they protested. I harnessed this feeling. Our class embarked on a research project. They chose to study Molly Brown, a local hero who survived the sinking of the *Titanic* and who was an early advocate for the rights of women, children, and laborers. My students wrote persuasive essays and successfully lobbied our principal to declare an official "Unsinkable Molly Brown Day" at our school.

Instead of dismissing my students' complaints, I leveraged their intolerance of injustice a second time when I invited all the girls to eat lunch in the classroom because there were issues with gossiping that needed to be addressed. The boys called me out. "That is not fair!" they accused with genuine and loud frustration. "It is not fair to treat people differently just because they are a boy or a girl." One student was actually screaming at me. I could have punished him for yelling, but I ended up conceding the point and invited the boys to eat lunch in the classroom the next day.

At my students' insistence, our class started both a "Gentleman's Lunch" and "Ladies' Lunch" program. Once a month, students who turn in their homework are rewarded with the opportunity to have lunch in their classroom with members from the community who act as role models and mentors. Our girls have had lunch with accountants and computer programmers, and our boys have eaten lunch with architects and financial managers. Since I was able to see their interest in equality as a resource, my students inspired a program that will leave a legacy at our school and contribute in meaningful ways to all the classes that follow theirs.

Acknowledging the resources our students come to school with is essential to empowering them to find success. Equally important is looking at the barriers they encounter as they come through our doors each day. Instead of thinking, "That kid never turns in homework," we should ask what the source of this issue is. With some conversation and investigation, a teacher can spot the source of the struggle and help the child solve the problem.

We cannot go home with our students and sit them down and force them to do a math worksheet, but we can help them understand the best time to start their homework, identify a good place to study, and seek out family and neighbors able to support them.

I encourage you to create a resource and barrier analysis for your students and your school as a whole. Then ask a simple question: "How can we use each student's gifts to help our school?" Next, ask yourself, "What can the school do to tear down some of the barriers that exist?" Each child and each school community will have different resources to build on and different barriers to address, but thinking along these lines will help start a conversation, which will empower your students.

2. Food Drawers and Coat Closets

I am proud to work at a school that is proactive in addressing food insecurity as an academic issue. As a part of our school's fight against hunger, a grant program has made it possible to provide our students with a real fruit snack each day. Our students come to count on this. "Miss, is it time for the nectarines?" is music to my ears. Additionally, our school participates in a program called Totes of Hope. Each week volunteers pick up canned food from the Food Bank of the Rockies and pack tote bags full of food to send home to fifty families who have expressed a need for food. These steps help bridge the gap for students.

Even with all these procedures in place, I still have students who have immediate food needs. I have a simple solution to address this: a food drawer. In my first year, I publicly passed out granola bars when children complained of rumbling tummies or fatigue. That was until one student, Jimmi, threw it back at me and said, "I don't need this, leave me alone." I realized that he was indeed hungry, but by placing a granola bar on his desk, I had effectively announced to the class that he did not have enough food at home. This is another example of my good intentions missing the mark of meeting a student's needs. Not having access to food is never a child's fault, but it does cause real feelings of embarrassment and shame. Jimmi taught me that if I wanted to address issues of hunger in my classroom, I needed to take a different approach.

I started a food drawer. I keep it stocked with snacks I buy myself or friends and family donate. I let my students know they can take what they need, no questions asked. My students are stealthy about it and grab food without my even noticing. This allows students to eat in class or even to sneak into the bathroom and eat secretly. Sometimes they eat a granola bar at recess and say they brought it from home; other times they take graham crackers home in their backpacks.

There are many iterations of the food drawer. Some programs, such as Feeding America's Food Pantry Program, complement their FRL meal programs with convenient food pantries located on-site at schools. I know one high school principal who hosted what he called the Peanut Butter Club that consisted of a few loaves of bread and jars of peanut butter and jelly that students could help themselves to when they needed it.

There are millions of teachers who have stepped in and fed hungry students, a fact that makes me proud of my profession. We truly are first responders. Many teachers ensure that food is available for their students when they need it, because a hungry student is not a student who can learn at his or her best.

Similarly, a freezing cold child cannot play. In Colorado, it gets cold. On the coldest days, when teachers and students alike lament that a snow day was not given, some of my students come to school in inadequate clothing, wearing sandals to walk through the snow or a thin sweatshirt in bitter cold. Our school has a coat closet, or rather several cardboard boxes shoved under a table, to respond to this need. We get these coats in many ways. Our local news affiliate, 7News, sponsors a citywide coat drive every year. Other times, neighborhood churches or families donate jackets. In 2015, complete strangers donated forty-two winter jackets to our students through a request I made on DonorsChoose.org.

Still, I have a bigger vision for our coat closet. I would love for our school to organize a coat swap where families could bring in outgrown jackets and shoes and swap them for better-fitting coats brought in by another family. I would love to see a "coat store" in the spirit of the Christmas Store program run by Mile High Ministries here in Denver. For twenty-three years, the Christmas Store has partnered with families in need to provide Christmas presents to kids. Referred families pick out and pay for gifts at steeply discounted prices. In this way the school can empower the community to use its own resources to meet its own needs, and with a little help and facilitation, families can provide warm clothes for their children.

In the end, our schools need to recognize that students come to us with needs that must be met for learning to occur. The needs your students display might be different from mine. Your students might need calculators to do their homework, or backpacks. Adolescent girls might need access to feminine hygiene products. Some families might need help facilitating transportation to and from school.

As teachers we can find ways to fill the gaps for our students. Talking about it is certainly easier than doing it, but find out what your students need and then find ways to connect them with resources and support. When our schools take steps to meet the needs of our students in every aspect of their lives, we ensure they have the resources to learn.

While we are doing all this hard work, we need to ensure that the reality we see is not hidden by the walls of our classrooms. Our governments, our school districts, and the public need to know what it is really like to be a student living in poverty, so they can enact policies and deliver services that support our students. This is not something over and above the scope of our duty as educators. It is our duty.

3. Community Supplies

At the beginning of the school year, teachers across America pass out lists of school supplies that families are expected to purchase for their children. But have you ever figured out how much it costs to buy all the supplies you put on your list? How much exactly? How much will that pack of markers cost if the family can't shop around for the best price? How much will a binder cost if the only store a family has access to is a local drugstore? For older students, do you know the cost of supplies for their combined classes? If you don't know, you should.

As a former student candidly put it, "The problem wasn't the one spiral notebook my history teacher said I needed. It was that every class asked for one. With three kids in our family, it would have been thirty dollars' worth of notebooks. That was the cost of one of our bills. So, every day I said I forgot my

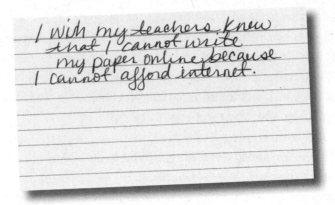

I wish my teachers knew that I cannot write my paper online because I cannot afford internet.

notebook and asked my friends to rip out a page for me. It was embarrassing."

As a child, I never knew how much school supplies cost. Not having access to school supplies was never an issue for me growing up and I gave little thought to it. Like many teachers, I typed up my list of requested supplies and sent it home with students at the beginning of each school year. The policy of a neighboring school, College View Elementary, caused me to rethink my approach. Teachers there do not send long lists of school supplies home with kids. They simply ask each family to contribute a set amount, like $20.

At first that seemed like a lot to me, but then I started asking my students' parents how much they currently paid for school supplies. I'm sure it is not shocking to anyone who has ever taken that crumpled school supply list to the store, but I was surprised when parents told me they were spending $70 to $80 to purchase all the listed supplies for just one student in my class. The numbers parents reported to me are blown out of the water by the Backpack Index annually compiled by Huntington Bank. In 2015, they found that the average cost for supplies and extracurricular school activities for an elementary school student was $649. For middle school students it was $941 and for high school students the cost was $1,402.

In light of this, my grade-level team decided to try the "we get the supplies" approach and families unanimously love it. On the family's end, they save time and money. On my end, as a teacher I can get the exact supplies that work for my class. And when I'm buying for thirty students I can get a much better deal. Plus, a class set of rulers or scissors can last years without my having to repurchase.

In addition, all the supplies in my classroom are "community supplies," which means we pool the pencils and crayons in one place so they are available for everyone. This helps create a sense of community and teaches students about shared resources. If one students bites off the erasers from all the pencils (and, yes, this has happened!) then the whole class is affected. On a more practical level, having community supplies cuts down on waste. Glue sticks go dry less often when we all take care of them.

Similarly, our basketball team requests a "recommended donation" instead of a sign-up fee. Families are also happy to contribute in nonmonetary ways by washing uniforms or setting out chairs before our games. Most students turn in the recommended donation, but another remarkable thing happens. Without any solicitation, some families give over and above the recommended donation and cover the costs of students not able to contribute any funding. It is another example of the community supporting itself.

The idea of community supplies may not be revolutionary, but I hope it illuminates how teachers can examine age-old school policies in order to make meaningful changes. I encourage you to try out the technique of community supplies. Small but important changes like this one, when added up, challenge the status quo and support our students.

4. Breakfast in the Classroom

Another age-old practice that is beginning to be reexamined is how we serve children food. Many of my students have enough food at home, but the truth is so many children in my classroom do not have the food they need to fuel their bodies. I have students whose only meals are provided at school, which means that after lunch their next meal is breakfast the following day. That is if they actually eat those meals.

Through the school lunch program, schools are able to provide both free lunches and free breakfasts to students who qualify and have completed the necessary paperwork. At our school in particular, we knew students in need were eating lunch, but few were eating breakfast. When we examined the issue more closely, we realized there were significant barriers to our students getting access to breakfast.

First, breakfast was served before school, so if students wanted to eat they had to arrive early. Second, when students arrived at school they were given the option of going into the cafeteria and eating breakfast or going outside and playing with their friends before the school bell rang. As you may guess, many kids chose to skip cereal and a banana in order to play tetherball. That choice might mean a six-year-old could be hungry and unfocused for an entire morning of learning. The final barrier was social. Even though so many of our students struggled with food insecurity, very few felt comfortable exposing themselves as being in need. By being one of the few students to go through the food line at breakfast, students publicly admitted they were hungry.

In 2010, some of these barriers to eating breakfast were removed for our nation's students. Legislators reauthorized the National School Lunch Program and titled it the Healthy, Hunger-Free Kids Act. One key component was updating the nutritional requirements, but the act also included the Community Eligibility Provision that "allows high-poverty schools to offer breakfast and lunch free of charge to all students." Any individual school, group of schools, or entire school district with 40 percent or more of students who are "already identified," meaning their family already receives government assistance, can participate in this program. But it is optional, which means that for many students nothing changed.

In 2013, Colorado's state legislature followed the lead of states like Texas and Arkansas and passed a bill mandating breakfast and lunch be universally offered in schools like mine that have 80 percent or more students qualifying for FRL. In addition, breakfast would be served after the school bell rang.

With this policy change, I saw the impact on my students' learning firsthand. My students can now eat breakfast in our classroom under the Breakfast in the Classroom model, which means all of my students are eating a nutritious morning meal every day.

Our school went from serving less than 200 breakfast meals a day to serving more than 450 breakfast meals a day. Think about that impact! That's more than 250 students eating breakfast each day who might not have eaten before. On any given morning in my classroom, you will see focused students flipping the pages of their books as they methodically munch on an apple. The ripple effects go beyond quieting the rumbling in their bellies. I now send fewer students to the school nurse with stomachaches or headaches, which means more student learning time. Students have also learned responsibility and teamwork by setting up and cleaning up after their daily community meal.

Research on the impact of Breakfast in the Classroom com-piled by the Food Research and Action Center confirms my observations. They cite studies that found "students with im-proved nutrient intake as a result of a program of school break-fast offered free to all students report decreases in symptoms of hunger." The impact of these programs extends even further: students who participate in breakfast programs show "greater improvements in math scores, attendance, punctuality, depres-sion, anxiety, and hyperactivity."

Most of my Teacher Tools focus on strategies teachers can implement in their classrooms, and I understand that rolling out a Breakfast in the Classroom program will take a collab-orative effort by an entire school or community. But I feel so passionately about this program that I want every teacher who serves students struggling with food insecurity to advocate for it in their classrooms, especially since the Community Eligibil-ity Provision gives schools a real opportunity to serve students better.

As schools, we are perfectly positioned to fight childhood hunger. I encourage teachers and schools to investigate the re-alities of food insecurity among their students and treat it as the learning problem it is. As teachers, let's use our voices to advocate for the barriers to healthful meals to be broken down and eliminated.

5. Empathetic Questions, Individualized Interventions

One year around the holidays, a community member offered to "adopt a family" and buy them Christmas presents. When our school psychologist called the family to find out what type of presents they would like, she asked the mother to think of something for herself. The mother replied, "Laundry detergent." As it turned out, one of her children, who had significant physical needs, often wet the bed. She did not have enough laundry detergent to wash the soiled sheets and to also wash the children's school clothes. Unintentionally, we had discovered that the root cause of her children's frequent absences from school was as simple as her not being able to wash their clothes. This taught me an important lesson about asking empathetic questions.

When our students struggle in school, we need to find the root of the problem, and to do this the first step is often asking an empathetic question. Think of a child who arrives late to school. Greeting the child with disappointment, hostility, or sarcasm makes the child feel they are the problem.

A true inspiration in my life as an educator is local hero Emily Griffith, who started an innovative school in Denver in 1908 "for all who wish to learn," which still survives today. In her Opportunity School she hung a sign that read ENTER YOUR CLASSES WHENEVER YOU CAN GET HERE. WE KNOW YOU TRY TO BE ON TIME. If educators start with a "we know you try" attitude we can work from this place to solve the problem. We must try to seek understanding and provide the necessary support, instead of automatically being punitive.

We teachers should work to discover the root cause of why a student is tardy. Focus on identifying what has become a barrier for the student. It could be as simple as "What makes it hard to get to school on time?" This question is solution focused instead of accusatory. There is a big difference between that and "Why are you always late?" If you want to know what circumstances are contributing to a problem, a good rule of thumb is to take the "you" out of the question.

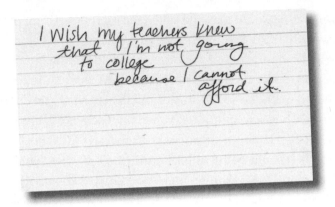

I wish my teachers knew that I'm not going to college because I cannot afford it.

Asking an empathetic question often provides a wealth of information. Maybe the student does not have reliable transportation to school. As the teacher, you can help facilitate a carpool or help figure out a bus route. Perhaps the child just needs help waking up. The school might be able to provide an alarm clock, find an app that can play a loud alarm, or ask a reliable neighbor to knock on their apartment door in the morning. Maybe the child needs earplugs so they can get a restful night's sleep. You can see how asking empathetic questions can open up a world of solutions adaptable to individual needs.

Poverty manifests itself in different ways. Geography, family dynamics, availability of resources, and each family's strengths can all dramatically impact a student's experiences. Even within the same community, one student's needs can be vastly different from another's. We cannot find out what supports each of our students needs until we have the right information.

Most of my students, like more than half of all children in American schools, live in poverty. Beyond lacking certain resources, this truth takes a very real emotional and physical toll. But let me be perfectly clear: there is no need to feel sorry for my students. My eight-year-old students perform Shakespeare, write computer code, and launch citywide book-drive campaigns. Each student in my classes, year after year, has enormous potential. I wholeheartedly believe a day will come when I will be working for one of my students or even voting for one of them.

As teachers, we need to continuously avoid the temptation to make assumptions and instead take active steps to understand our students' lives. Teachers play an important role when we educate ourselves in the realities our students face when they live in poverty. We can equip ourselves with knowledge of how poverty in American schools fits into a national context, and we can become advocates to provide the resources and support our students need.

Teachers are truly on the front lines of poverty. We have a responsibility to do everything we can to ensure all of our students have equal access to a quality education. Understanding the realities of our students' lives may not always be comfortable for everyone, but facing these issues head on is the best way to understand and help our students. If our good intentions backfire, we need to reflect and make improvements.

As individual teachers, we may feel that the scope of poverty is too big and anything we do will barely make a dent. But when you consider that each of us has the opportunity to affect and improve the lives of so many children each school year, it's easy to see how our collective impact could change the world. But it's up to each of us, in every classroom, to work toward that change.

she broke my heart when she declared that my art isn't good enough.

that it was difficult to pay attention in class, not drawing, while I was going to sleep at night.

I wish my teacher knew that I've lived a hard life and I try my hardest and best to remain positive every second of the day

I WISH MY TEACHER KNEW I love my family

I wish my te... at my mom an... a argument ev... effect me an... ren they do... lled and my...

...r knew th... ...le to ache...

I wish my teacher knew that moving schools its ...rd to make friends with people you feel don't ...e you.

...r knew ...my mom might got diagnos... with cancer this week and I... been without a home 3 dif... times this year alone.

I WISH MY TEACHER KNEW I love my family

I wish my teacher knew that I hated to go back to the chu... every night & it was difficult to pay attention in class

...wish my teacher knew that ...metimes my feelings and ...otions are already crushed when ...alk into class and he/she ...akes it worse by being hostile

I WISH MY TEACHER KNEW I love my...

...o not pressure kids when they ...n't know what's going on at ...me.

3.

All Families Count
Including Families in
All Their Forms

When it comes to families, our classrooms play a major role in reflecting the larger culture and accepted norms. Family plays an essential role in all children's lives and therefore families, in all their forms, need to be included in every classroom.

Creating a classroom environment that does not merely tolerate all families but actively includes every definition of a family helps students feel valued and supported. I strive to move my classroom away from a culture of allowing for perceived abnormalities into a classroom culture where all families are universally included.

Let's be clear. The ideal of a Norman Rockwell family with a mom, dad, two kids, and a dog that was once prominent in our country is not the reality for the majority of Americans. Between the 2000 and 2010 US Censuses, husband-wife family households continued a downward trend and officially became the minority, with only 48.4 percent of families having this traditional makeup.

Modern families exist in a variety of forms. According to the *New York Times*, families are more "ethnically, racially, religiously, and stylistically diverse than a half generation ago—than even a half year ago." Consider these statistics: More than 40 percent of American babies are born to single mothers. Gay and lesbian parents are becoming more common; recent estimates show that one out of every thirty-seven children goes home to two moms or two dads. The number of unmarried yet cohabiting parents is rising as marriage rates decline.

And some family units aren't technically "family" by traditional definitions. When I worked in District of Columbia Public Schools, the idea of "play cousins" was prominent. Even though two children were not biological cousins, this term was used to describe a stronger bond than that of just friend or neighbor. In my school, it is now common for my students to describe older females close to the family as *tías*, or "aunties," even if it is not technically true.

A recent study at the University of Puget Sound explored how over one hundred participants developed deep relationships and ties to people who weren't blood relatives. The researchers found that there are several types of so-called voluntary kin who can constitute a family. Although not technically "kin" by law or genetics, these types of relationships can be just as real and meaningful to students as they might be with blood relatives.

Another way a family makeup can change is through divorce. Recent statistics cited in the *New York Times* and the *Huffington Post* demonstrate the divorce rate is on the decline and could dip as low as 30 percent due to several factors; these include cohabitation before marriage, couples choosing to cohabit instead of getting married, and delaying marriage until

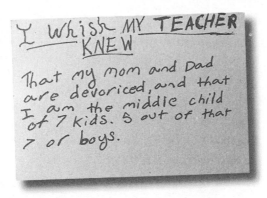

I Whish MY TEACHER KNEW

That my mom and Dad are devoriced, and that I am the middle child of 7 kids. 5 out of that 7 or boys.

couples are in their midtwenties or later. Teachers need to be aware that students being raised by a married couple is not a given.

Marriage may not be part of a student's home life, and a biological relationship to a parent might not be either. Consider the rise of students who live in adoptive homes. In 2014, The US Department of State reported that 6,441 children were adopted from abroad. The Congressional Coalition Adoption Institute also compiles statistics on adoption and foster care. They state that "adopted children make up roughly 2 percent of the total child population under the age of 18."

For some students, the status of their family can be changing and transitional. Every September 30, the US Department of Health and Human Services takes a count of children in foster care. The number has been trending upward. In 2014, there were 415,129 children in foster care and 66 percent of them were school age. For some of these children, a foster care placement may lead to a permanent home, but for more than half, the stated goal in their case plan is to return to the custody of their parents or primary caregiver. This means that not only are there a lot of children in our schools who go home to a foster

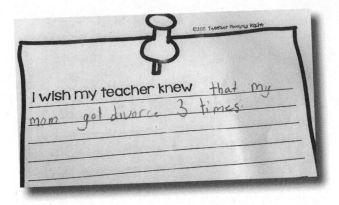

family, but also there are a lot of children whose placement in that family is likely to change.

The traditional definition of family doesn't always fit these students, but there are moves teachers can make to support them. The most important step to support all forms of families is to ask students what their family looks like. Allow students to define their family. Instead of asking questions that make assumptions about a family, leave them open-ended. Simply saying, "Tell me about your family," "Who lives in your home?" "Is there anyone you can read with at home?" instead of asking, "Does your dad live with you?" or "Is he your real brother?" will allow students to speak freely about their family situations without having to correct your understanding of family.

Included Families Can Become Involved Families

It's important to include family in all its forms at school, because research has overwhelmingly shown that the more involved a student's family is with their education, the more likely it is the student will perform well in school, graduate from high school, and even attend college. In fact, a study conducted by Stanford Center for the Study of Families, Children, and Youth demonstrated that when adult family members were involved in the decisions an adolescent student made about school, the result was more academic effort and better grades for the student regardless of gender, sex, ethnicity, or social status.

In order to include all families, our schools need to engage all families. Leading researchers in this area, Anne T. Henderson and Karen L. Mapp, outlined six major action steps to establishing effective family engagement programs in schools:

1. Recognize that all parents, regardless of income, education level, or cultural background are involved in their children's education and want their children to do well in school;
2. Link family and community engagement efforts to student learning;
3. Create initiatives that will support families to guide their children's learning, from preschool through high school;
4. Develop the capacity of school staff to work with families;
5. Focus efforts to engage families on developing trusting and respectful relationships; and
6. Embrace a philosophy of partnership and be willing to share power with families. Make sure that parents and school staff understand that the responsibility for children's educational development is a collaborative enterprise.

These recommendations speak to a school's philosophy about making families meaningful partners in students' education. These are big-picture ideas, and they can gain traction when attitudes about including all families trickle down to individual classrooms, individual teachers, even individual lessons.

Don't be squeamish about bringing the idea of family into your lessons. I teach a powerful lesson each year where students identify the habits of good readers by describing the best reader they know, which almost always ends up being a parent or sibling. After you find out more about your students' families you can include family members' names in math problems. Find opportunities for students to authentically communicate with their families. This can even be done on the fly.

One day in class, my lesson plan was to summarize a book about tide pools. One student commented, "My grandmother lives next to tide pools in Mexico." Immediately we changed our summary paragraph into a letter to his grandmother so we could tell her what we had learned. We still summarized the text, but it was so much more meaningful to write to a family member.

The definition of family is different for every child. The reality of modern American families is that there is no norm; there is no one perfect family. If we are to leverage the power of families in our classrooms, we must ensure that all families are included.

Diversity in Families

All schools and educators should work to include families in every form. But equally as important is including families who come from diverse backgrounds and cultures. The issue of how cultural and socioeconomic diversity influence learning is a topic worthy of deep exploration by researchers and educators alike. How to best support diverse families could make up a whole book, and has.

But all teachers can observe and analyze the cultural and ethnic backgrounds that make up their individual school com-

> – I wish my teacher knew that i got kicked out of the house because of my moms girlfriend, and now i don't have a relationship with my mom because of it

munity. In my experience, even when a school community seems relatively homogeneous, there are always families with different situations, backgrounds, and experiences present. For example, my school serves nearly 90 percent of students and families who identify as Latino. Yet within that group there are families from different cultural experiences, families with multiple children, families from recent immigrant backgrounds, and families dealing with housing insecurity. Despite having similar cultural identities on paper, families at my school observe different holidays, hold various belief systems, and have a wide range of schedules and priorities. Each family can present different strengths and barriers to interacting with teachers and the school community.

Taking a critical look at the families who make up our schools helps educators determine what kinds of support are most needed, as well as how to better leverage the resources each family can contribute to the overall school community. There is no one best way to connect with families, which is why teachers and schools should offer a variety of opportunities for families to meaningfully participate in their child's education, both inside and outside the school environment.

Teacher Tools

1. Inclusive Family Language

Inclusive family language can mean the difference between students feeling alone or different, and students feeling their family experience is validated.

Allow students to self-identify who their family is. It is important, as teachers, not to get hung up on the actual biological definition of family. Don't correct students; allow students to be in control of who gets designated as "family." Be inclusive of what a family is or means to students.

Once I had to intervene in a classroom argument between two students who were arguing about who was allowed to be a "twin." One girl who actually had a twin brother had a second student on the verge of tears, telling her that she was not allowed to have a twin. The second girl had a cousin of the same age who frequently lived in the same home and her family always called them "twins." I explained that in our classroom family was a status, not a person. Anyone who cares about you deeply could be called your family. In that way, our whole classroom acts as a family.

Being deliberate about using inclusive family language can help all students feel they belong in your classroom. One recommendation from the School of Education at the University of Delaware is to "review forms and regulations that demonstrate a bias towards intact families. Such policies discriminate and embarrass single parents and children of divorce."

A first and quick swap for teachers is to swap the word "parent" for "family." Think about all the little things we say: "Tell your parents about the field trip" or "Have your parents sign this." The word "parent" is everywhere in our classrooms. Even as I wrote this I realized that my reading homework had a box for "parent signature." The good news is that this was a quick fix. I timed it for you all. It took me forty-four seconds to change the homework to simply read "signature."

Then there is the institution of the "parent-teacher conference." It is so important for teachers to meet regularly with a student's family, and in some cases this term is accurate: a student's parents come in to confer with me, the teacher. Yet I often meet with a student's aunt, uncle, or older sibling. Sometimes I meet with grandparents, foster parents, or other caregivers. Changing the name to "family school conference" is so simple. So simple, in fact, that I emailed my principal and did it. Here is the email I sent her:

Subject: Quick Thought
Hi Jo,
As I am doing research for this book, I had an idea. Looking at the actual makeup of families, I thought it might be a small but important step to change the way we, at Doull, refer to "Parent-Teacher Conferences" to "Family School Conferences." What do you think?
Thanks,
Kyle

And here is her response:

Re: Quick Thought
That's a GREAT idea!! LOVE IT!
Jo Carrigan, Principal

I felt so empowered that this change was made in my school that I set about making this inclusive family language benefit

Family Language	It's inclusive. Keep it!	Not inclusive. Change it to:
Parent-Teacher Conferences		
Parent-Teacher Association		
Collaborative School Committee		
Daddy-Daughter Dance		
Family Art Night		
Mother's Day Crafts		
Parent or Guardian		

more students. I sent a similar email to my superintendent, and within a few hours the chief officer of Family and Community Engagement replied and agreed to make the change in terminology on official documents. Like most larger school districts, we have an entire department dedicated to including and engaging families in school life, but sometimes it takes one of us teachers who is face to face with students every day to advocate for these changes. We teachers can make big impacts advocating for inclusive family language.

These are small but important changes. Some people might argue that this is simply political correctness and that schools are being overly sensitive in making these changes. I argue that students learn best when they feel they belong; when they can see tangible evidence that their home life is accepted and validated by their school.

I encourage teachers either individually or collaboratively to look at all the ways their schools describe families. Really investigate all the groups, organizations, events, and even the terms on forms. Find all the language we use to speak about families and create a simple chart like the one on the previous page to help guide your thinking.

It is worth our time to have a conversation about the language we use when we refer to families. If it is inclusive, keep it. However, if the language we use is not inclusive, if it does not reflect the actual lives of students who attend our schools or could attend in the future, we owe it to our students to discuss what changes need to be made.

2. How Many Family Groups?

Every school year there are several students in my classroom who split their time between different homes. Sometimes this is the effect of divorce or a family separation; sometimes it is a practical solution to dividing up the care of children. Other times students in my classes spend much of their time with a grandparent who would also like to be involved in school events. In these situations, communication between the school and families can become complicated.

A simple yet often neglected question to ask is, "How many family groups do you have?" This can be asked in person or on a beginning-of-the-year survey that is sent home. I like the wording of this question because it does not presuppose that students are part of a traditional nuclear family; it leaves room for students to define their own family.

I used to feel a little squeamish about asking my students clarifying questions about the structures of their families, afraid to step on toes or offend, but I have found there is no need to feel this way. If I am unclear, there is certain to be misunderstanding during the school year, but when I understand a family's structures and preferences, I can meet a student's needs better.

Understanding how a student's family is structured can be valuable to a teacher in several ways. Knowing how many family groups a student is part of can help a teacher know how to schedule conferences so that everyone is included, or to know the best person to call when a problem arises at school.

On the most basic level, teachers can communicate better with families when they understand the different family dynamics in their classroom. I know how many field trip announcements and picture-day reminders to send home. Especially in elementary school, communication from the school is often sent home in a take-home folder. Some of my students spend a week in their mother's home and the following week in the father's home. In these cases I simply make two folders. For example, several of my students have one folder marked "For Mom" and another marked "For Dad." Just sending home communication to all the family groups the student interacts with can help ease tensions in a family and keep everyone informed of what is going on at school.

Another benefit of knowing how many family groups a student is a part of concerns sending work home. When I send home a student's completed work, I include special instructions. I say to my students, "You worked hard on this essay and it deserves to be displayed! Your job is to show this to someone important and hang it up in an important place." One day a student reported that she hung her essay on the front door of her apartment so everyone in the building could read it.

If I know that a student has two or three homes, that's two or three refrigerators and doors on which their work could be proudly displayed. As a teacher, it doesn't take much effort to print out an extra student essay or make a few extra copies of a student's work. Sometimes I will just ask kids to hold up on their fingers how many copies of their work they need.

It's meaningful to parents and caregivers to have access to their student's work. And for students who split their time between several homes, it can provide a small yet important sense of consistency. No matter where a child sleeps on a particular night, their work can be proudly displayed everywhere they call home.

3. Daily CQC: Celebrations, Questions, Concerns

Every day I try to make time in my day for CQC, a time when students can share celebrations, questions, or concerns with the class. I got this idea from our school's staff meetings, during which our principal would open up the floor for teachers to share whatever was on their minds. I thought my students would like the same opportunity, so I started a daily CQC.

To run a CQC with your class all you need is to ask a simple question: "Does anyone have a celebration, question, or concern to share?" I invite students to share about things happening at school and happening at home, then watch eager hands shoot up. If students seem reluctant, I share my own CQC, which has always been enough to encourage students to share.

My students tell our classroom community about anything they think is important in their lives, which means I learn what kids really care about. They tell me about soccer games and new movies coming out. It helps me understand what makes each student tick. One year, a student updated me every day about the ranking of NFL teams, which told me I could use football as a motivator. We began calling our 7s multiplication tables the "touchdown tables."

CQC is a particularly good opportunity for students to let our class know what is happening in their families. Often I will hear a countdown to a birthday: "My baby brother's birthday is in seventeen days." Or, "We are moving into a new apartment and I am going to get a bunk bed!" Students can opt in, and they can also choose if they want to share something exciting or something they are worried about.

In this way, I have been able to learn about changes in my students' families. A student once shared, "I'm sad today because my sister and my mom got in a fight and now my sister moved away." I've also heard, "My mom and Eduardo are getting married and I get to wear a suit." Another student informed the class, "My mom moved to California, but she is coming back for my birthday and we are going to an amusement park." With students sharing about their individual circumstances, it proves to the whole class that family comes in many forms.

All this information helps me be a better teacher to each student. I can understand certain sensitivities they might have or situations that might trigger an emotional reaction. But the support offered is not just top down, from teacher to student; the students in our class support each other. Our class can celebrate together during the good times, like wishing a friend good luck on their baseball tournament. When a student shares a challenge, their classmates can be there to offer support.

When a student shares a concern they have, like "I miss my dad," I acknowledge and accept their feelings. I confirm that their situation is real and difficult, and resist the urge to offer advice or figure out a solution. Many times a student is really seeking to be heard rather than having their problem fixed. Sometimes other students have dealt with the same issue and offer kind words. It is empowering for a student who has also struggled with a parent not able to be present to share thoughts or encouragement that can help one of their peers. I always elicit an expression from our class community. I will say, "It's tough, but no matter what . . ." and our class chimes in ". . . we got your back."

Getting to know students can happen in many different ways. For older students, CQC could be something written down on notes to the teacher. I have seen teachers use Twitter in the classroom to have students share this information. Whatever form CQC takes, asking students about their lives and genuinely listening without judgment will help promote a strong community in your classroom.

4. Reimagining the Family Project

Including family into our lessons is a wonderful way to connect students' learning to the real world. All forms of families are valued and able to participate.

The Family Tree is an age-old school project, and it does have a few benefits. It helps children understand the concept of generations and visualize connections and relationships, but the traditional family tree chart falls short in many other ways. To begin with, the family tree is out of date. Popularized in the eighteenth century as a way for young women to practice their needlework, the traditional family tree has not evolved to fit the realities of a modern family. The format itself is constraining, and we know it does not represent the majority of American children's family experience.

If a teacher feels strongly about utilizing the Family Tree in class, consider a few options that would be inclusive for all forms of families. One idea is to allow students to either use their actual family, or a family from literature or a TV show. Even coming up with a fictional family allows students to complete the assignment in a way that feels comfortable. If the objective of the Family Tree is to simply display a family, teachers can invite students to complete a Family Wheel with different sections for each family member, or even a Family Constellation where many family groups can exist with equal importance.

There are many other family projects that can be reimagined. Be deliberate in considering ways a lesson or project can be inclusive. There is a common Montessori lesson teachers use to celebrate birthdays. Students hold a globe and walk around a candle to represent that the Earth completes one revolution around the sun for each year of a child's life. Traditionally, students bring in a picture from each year of their lives. It helps them understand time sequence and connect the passage of time with the movement of the planets. But the problem is that not all children, particularly children who have been adopted, have access to such pictures. Director and teacher at Family Montessori of Lebanon in Ohio, Erica Nichols (who also happens to be my cousin) makes this simple change. "Instead of baby pictures for this lesson, our classroom chooses to use an event which took place each year in the child's life, like when a student broke their arm or their favorite football team won the Super Bowl. There are simple changes I can make to existing lessons so that all our students feel like their family experiences are valued. For me, it's worth it to think my lessons through and make sure all of my students and their families are included."

Another consideration is how our classrooms celebrate holidays. For many students, Mother's Day and Father's Day are wonderful times to celebrate family members. But the truth is that these days can carry a different meaning for many students. Our schools, especially our elementary schools, would do well to think through celebrations like Mother's Day or Father's Day. Often there are lovely books to be read and crafts to make on these days, but it might also mean that some students in your room are left out or feel like the exception. There are ways to make crafts and honor special people in our students' lives without assuming that each student has a mother or father to be celebrated.

Reflecting on how our classroom projects and lessons fit into our students' understanding of family helps all students participate fully. We teachers are creative, and a little consideration about how to make these projects open and inclusive to more students can mean the world to them.

I'm sure there are some who would say making changes to the language we use to refer to families or family-centered projects is unnecessary. Perhaps there are some who think there is a singular definition of family all children should fit into. As a teacher you can expect this response and expect some to continue to do things the way they have always been done. But we owe it to our students to allow the realities of their lives to be represented in their learning. Like the American family itself, our thinking can evolve. It is worth the effort to include families because all students, all families, can be powerful forces in a child's education when they feel they are accepted and included.

wish my teacher knew what
she broke my heart when
she declared that my
art isn't good enough.

wish my teacher knew
that it was difficult to pay atten
in class, not knowing where I was
going to sleep at night

wish mu
eacher
new I
ve my
=amil

I wish my teacher knew that
I've lived a hard life and I try
my hardest and best to remain
positive every second of the da

I wish my teacher knew
My dad died this year, I feel more
alone/ disconnected from my peers than
ever before.

Brittney, 6th grade

I wish my teacher knew
my mom might get diagnosed
with cancer, this week and I've
been without a home 3 di
times this year alone.

wish my teacher knew
hat moving schools its
ard to make friends
ith people you feel don't
e you.

I wish my teacher knew that
I hated to go back to the scho
y night & it was difficult to
attention in class

wish my teacher knew that
metimes my feelings and
notions are already crushed when
walk into class and he/she
akes it worse by being hostil

to not pressure kids when they
ont know what's going on at
ome.

I wish
teacher
knew I
Love bac

4.
We Will Get Through This Together
Supporting Students Through Grief and Loss

My Classroom Community

Simon started to shut down in class regularly. He would curl himself up in the tightest of balls and wriggle his way behind the computer cart or in between thick winter coats. I always wondered what he was thinking as he wrapped his lanky arms around his legs and rocked back and forth. Maybe he was perseverating on a difficult thought or maybe his mind was going completely blank as the gentle rocking soothed him. Either way, Simon was checked out of our classroom world, floating somewhere by himself.

The incidents that triggered this reaction were always small. Someone stepped on his shoe or another student cut in front of him in line. The truth was these little slights were not the cause of Simon's distress. I was told Simon's mother had moved to Nevada. Whether or not she would return was uncertain. Simon was grieving.

It took me months to figure out how to gently coax Simon back into our lessons. At first, nothing I did or said worked. I waited out his episodes. I attempted to bribe him with promises of free time. I gave him community incentives like earning the whole class extra recess, and I gave him access to calming activities. I also enlisted the aid of our school psychologist, who worked with Simon privately. Regardless of my approach, he would sit tightly woven in a ball, until one day I stumbled upon a strategy that broke him out of his guarded state.

Simon had wedged himself into a small space between the computer cart and the wall, making himself invisible. Instead of asking him to join the class, I said, "Simon, can you help me push in these chairs? The kids left them all a mess and I need your help." Taken off guard, he stood up and started pushing in the chairs with me. I showered him with praise: "Thank goodness you're here. This room would be such a disaster if we didn't have you helping us. We need you."

"Yes," he agreed. "These chairs really need to be pushed in. Everyone has just left this place a complete mess."

From then on, "Can you help me?" seemed like a secret password. Feeling that he was contributing seemed to lift Simon out of a dark place. I think that's because it made him feel he was needed and appreciated by the class. He knew our class could not function without him. The rest of the school year was not perfect, but he was always more engaged after he completed a task that helped the classroom, whether it was turning on lights or wiping off tables.

Simon found strategies that would help him bounce back after his emotions overwhelmed him, like taking deep breaths or finding a chair in a quieter place in the room. He still struggled at times, but I could see he was processing his grief and developing skills that would help him overcome this challenge.

As a teacher, it was essential for me to uncover the true cause of Simon's change in behavior. He was not following class rules, but not out of defiance. He was grieving. His refusal to participate in classroom activities and lessons was not something to take personally, because it was a cry for help. As teachers, we should work hard to recognize students' needs so we can help them through difficult times in their lives.

Childhood Grief and Mourning

Death and loss are difficult subjects to discuss, even with adults. For teachers, tackling these subjects with children is even more daunting. It can be a challenge to find the precise words to say, or know what supportive moves to make. Often our apprehension at broaching the subjects of grief and loss might cause us to avoid conversations that could be uncomfortable, so we do not respond at all. But it does not have to be this way.

As teachers we can learn how to support our students even through the most difficult times in their lives. In fact, it's imperative that we do so, because when a child is dealing with the negative spiral of grief and loss, that child is not in the best position to learn.

First, it's important for teachers to recognize that grief may be a response to something other than death. In children, grief might be the result of the absence of a parent due to many reasons, like divorce, deportation, incarceration, or abandonment. The loss of a pet can often be the source of grief for children;

so can changing homes. It may be easy for us adults to dismiss when it happens to children, but genuine grief can be the consequence of the ending of a romantic relationship or the conclusion of a friendship.

The process of dealing with that grief is called mourning, and it can last for varying degrees of time. The American Cancer Society explains mourning as the "outward expression of loss and grief. Mourning includes rituals and other actions that are specific to each person's culture, personality, and religion." Mourning is an important step and should not be rushed.

Every incident of death or loss is different. Therefore, every response will be equally unique. Some students may exhibit strong signs of anguish, while others might appear as though nothing happened. George Bonanno, a clinical psychologist at Columbia University and author of *The Other Side of Sadness,* has studied grief for over twenty years. Among his most provocative findings is that 50 to 60 percent of mourners show no symptoms of grief one month following the loss. Some even overcome the grief within days. Due to this spectrum of grief responses, it is important to give children the amount of time they need to mourn, and it is equally important to understand the variety of ways in which grief is displayed and experienced.

How Children Grieve

Due to the natural evolution of a child's development, their understanding of death and loss changes as they age. Young children can falsely interpret death as intentional abandonment or a temporary situation that can be reversed. One friend of mine remembers losing his father at seven years old. He waited each day for his father to return home, even though the adults in his life had told him his father had died. Since he was so young he did not comprehend what this meant. His understanding of death had been confused by seeing a character on a TV show die, then seeing the same actor miraculously appear on a different program. No one explained the difference to him, so he stared out the window for years searching for his father.

Children under the age of eight tend to be satisfied with a simple, clear explanation of death or loss. However, by the time a child is between the ages of eight and ten, they enter another development stage and their reaction may be different. Some children believe death won't happen to them, while for others a death in the family or the broader community can prompt intense curiosity and speculation. Children this age begin to look to adults for more nuanced answers to their questions.

However, during preadolescence and adolescence stages of development, most children depend on their peers for support as they build their own understanding of death and loss. At this stage, they begin to see life as finite. Some teens and tweens begin to build a spiritual belief system to help develop their understanding, while others become more likely to engage in high-risk behavior.

It's important to note that as children age, there may be additional periods of grieving even after the initial reaction is long past. For example, a child who experienced the loss of a close family member at a very young age might suddenly need support when they enter middle school, or become a teenager. I remember a high school classmate of mine experiencing deep sorrow over the loss of his sister who, sadly, had died at birth many years before. At the time, I didn't understand why he suddenly felt this way when the loss had occurred so many long ago, but when we understand how the developmental stages affect grief responses, we realize this is completely normal.

Know the Signs of Grief and Loss

The Dougy Center, the National Center for Grieving Children & Families, has compiled a list of common responses of the grieving child or teen for schools. The organization reminds teachers that "remembering that each person grieves differently, it is important for each student to feel heard and accepted" and advise, "each response should be accepted and allowed, as long as it is not harmful to the student or another person."

Academic Responses to Grief
- Difficulty focusing or concentrating, inattentiveness, daydreaming
- Failing or declining grades
- Incomplete work, or poor quality of work
- Increased absences or reluctance to go to school
- Forgetfulness, memory loss
- Overachievement, trying to be perfect
- Language errors and word-finding problems

Behavioral Responses to Grief
- Noisy outbursts, disruptive behaviors, "hyperactive-like" behavior
- Aggressive behaviors, frequent fighting
- Noncompliance to requests, "I don't care" attitude
- Isolation or withdrawal
- Increased need for attention

Emotional Responses to Grief
- Insecurity, issues of abandonment, safety concerns
- Concern about being treated differently than others
- Depression, hopelessness, intense sadness
- Overly sensitive, frequently tearful, irritable
- Regression to times when things felt safer and more in control
- Preoccupation with death, wanting details
- A need for checking in on surviving family members and friends
- Appears unaffected by the death

Social Responses to Grief
- Withdrawal from friends, activities, or sports
- Changes in relationships with teachers and peers
- Use of drugs or alcohol
- Inappropriate sexual behavior/acting out
- Stealing, shoplifting

Physical Responses to Grief
- Increased requests to visit the nurse
- Stomachaches, headaches, heartaches, hives, rashes, itching, nausea, upset stomach
- Increased illnesses, low resistance to colds and flu
- Loss of appetite or increased eating
- Low energy, weakness

How Common Is Grief?

The Children's Grief Awareness Day campaign released staggering statistics about just how many children experience grief and loss:

- One out of every 20 children aged fifteen and younger will suffer the loss of one or both parents.
- 1.5 million children are living in a single-parent household because of the death of one parent.
- One in five children will experience the death of someone close to them by age 18.
- One in every 1,500 secondary school students dies each year.
- It is estimated that 73,000 children die every year in the United States. Of those children, 83 percent have surviving siblings.

These numbers make it clear that teachers will inevitably teach students who are experiencing grief in their classrooms. But it's important to note that these particular statistics focus primarily on death as the instigating factor for grief. Since we know that grief responses can be triggered by other forms of loss, we must realize that the net grief casts in our classrooms stretches even wider. The Pew Charitable Trust found in 2010 that "1.2 million inmates—over half of the 2.3 million people behind bars—are parents of children under age 18." That means that a staggering one out of every twenty-eight children in the United States has a parent in prison." This does not account for the number of incarcerated siblings, close family members, or friends, which might also cause a student to grieve.

Additionally, separation from parents or family members due to immigration issues is another issue that can cause our students to experience grief and loss. When a parent is deported, some children accompany their parents out of the country and some stay here in American schools, sometimes entering into foster care. The Pew Research Center found that "children with at least one unauthorized immigrant parent made up 6.9 percent of students enrolled in kindergarten through 12th grade in 2012."

These statistics indicate that our classrooms serve many students who are grieving the loss of a loved one or living under the threat of losing a loved one. The unfortunate reality is that, for many reasons, our classrooms will have children who are grieving.

Transitioning Families and Grief

The students who enter our classrooms each day can also be shaped by grief and loss they have experienced in the context of a changing family. A transition in the family, like divorce or adoption, can cause grief.

According to *Scientific American,* every year 1.5 million school-aged students will experience the divorce of their parents. Psychologist and parenting expert Carl E. Pickhardt explains that children tend to react differently to divorce based on their age and maturity. Adolescents, who are already acting more independently of their parents, tend to "deal more aggressively with divorce, often acting in a mad, rebellious way." This might include acting out, disobeying rules, and being more selfish or self-involved.

In contrast, Pickhardt explains in *Psychology Today* that younger children are more dependent on their parents and because of that, can harbor hopes that everything will return to normal once their parents choose to love one another again. They might feel anxious and insecure about their world because it becomes difficult to predict what will happen on a day-to-day basis.

Essentially, divorce and separation can elicit "a more regressive response in the child and a more aggressive response in the adolescent," according to Pickhardt. Regardless of age, these responses can also affect learning. A 2011 study published in the *American Sociological Review* demonstrates how divorce can affect a child's ability to learn. Researchers found that children whose parents had divorced earned lower math scores during and after the divorce process. There was also a negative effect on interpersonal skills, such as the ability to make and maintain friendships. It's important to note that the researchers who conducted this particular study noted that the overall effect on children was limited. For example, reading test scores weren't affected by divorce.

Like divorce, adoption can dramatically change the shape of a family and cause some children to experience grief. Rachael Burnett Daugherty, MSW, is an adoption professional at an international adoption agency. She encourages teachers to put an adoptive child's experience in a broader context:

> There is no typical adoption. Adoption happens in many forms so each child's experience and reaction to that experience will be unique. Teachers should be aware that in some adoptions grief and loss can play a big role. Especially when a child's adoption experience causes emotional trauma during a crucial de-

velopmental stage. The legacy of this trauma can show up even years later. For example, if an adopted child is in the crucial stage between eight and ten years old and experiences a typical rejection from a peer, like being excluded from a lunch table, he or she might have what could appear to be an overreaction. A small incident like this could lead to a fight or an emotional outburst. A connection can be made from this negative behavior to the initial loss the child experienced being placed for adoption.

Regardless of what causes a child to suffer grief or loss, we should remember that the experience and trauma linger long after the actual event. If and when a student suddenly begins to "act out" or show dramatic changes in behavior, we teachers should ask ourselves, "Could the child's behavior be the result of grief?"

Supporting Students through the Grief Process

As much as we wish we could, protecting children from difficult circumstances such as death and loss is not possible. Nor is it beneficial for our students. We do them a better service when we acknowledge their grief and lead them to positive ways of dealing with the intense emotions that come along with it.

Our classrooms can become a supportive environment for students before and after a grief incident occurs. Openly discussing issues of death as they arise organically, such as when a class pet dies or when characters pass away in literature, helps our students understand that death is an appropriate topic. Academic subjects, such as life cycles, human anatomy, even many great works of literature, can become opportunities to develop

I wish my teacher knew that my cousin needs to go to the hospital when she does not feel good and I feel sad about her.

students' understanding of death. It is a natural part of life, and I think death can appear in the academic life of a classroom.

It's important that as teachers we know how to respond when a student has experienced grief or loss. Andrea Ruth Hopkins, MEd, early childhood educator with the Saint Paul Public Schools and grief facilitator, lays out three roles for educators responding to a grief or loss incident in their classroom:

1. To help children feel safe while acknowledging the reality of death
2. To promote an accepting classroom atmosphere where children's feelings are supported
3. To provide developmentally appropriate learning opportunities that allow children to discuss death.

Supporting a student through a traumatic event like a death may not be our area of expertise, but we need not be intimidated. Professor Linda Goldman offers this advice for teachers who are unsure of their role: "It is important for educators to be present with grieving students and encourage them to share where they are in their grief process and what they need. Have faith and trust in them. The children are the only ones that can relay their personal experience. Allow them to explore and express themselves freely."

She adds: "We as educators must create guidelines to aid children through their grief journey, protect them in school during vulnerable times and make their classroom an oasis of protection to explore life issues with support and guidance." Helping a student through grief can mean offering a listening ear, or an open door for questions. "When family, friends, and teachers rally around a student . . . The more caring adults on a student's team the better."

Teacher Tools

1. Tell the Truth

We need to be prepared to respond to our students' questions about grief and loss in a way that satisfies curiosity and fosters resiliency. When children ask questions about death or loss, they expect complete answers. When adults offer a restricted or limited answer—or, worst of all, no answer—most children will assume the topic is off-limits. Without an adult to turn to, a grieving child quickly can become isolated.

When a student asks you a question, take it seriously and answer it honestly. Try to avoid clichés about death. Children often take our words literally and this can cause confusion. Well-meaning but abstract euphemisms like "crossed over," "has gone away," or "went to sleep for a long time" could cause confusion and anxiety in a child. Even common phrases like "is watching over us" or "wanted to go to heaven" might unintentionally confound the issue if a child does not have a well-developed understanding of physical death. Ensure that the reality of the situation is made clear.

A good rule of thumb is to be direct and simple. Professor Goldman advises that "many children are comfortable with concise and truthful answers, especially at young ages. If explanations are too long or contain too much information, some children may tune out the conversation." There are no categorically right or wrong ways of talking to a child about death or loss. But when a child asks a difficult question about death, it's best to answer in age-appropriate, deliberately clear language.

Though the chart on the next page is adapted from Professor Goldman's book *Great Answers to Difficult Questions about Death,* it is far from a comprehensive list of questions your students may ask, or answers you might give. But I hope it empowers you to have open conversations with them. I know I feel better knowing I have a few simple sentences in my toolbelt to use when students ask difficult questions without much warning.

For example, one day during CQC (my daily meeting with students where they can share a celebration, question, or concern) a wide-eyed student shot her hand up in the air and said, "I have a concern. Can cancer kill you? My grandma has cancer and I want to know if she will die." It was quite a weighty question for a Monday afternoon, but I was able to give an answer.

I stuck with my plan and was simple and honest. "Sometimes cancer does kill people, but other times people with cancer can live for a long time. It usually depends what kind of cancer a person has and how quickly a doctor can treat it. I don't know about your grandma's cancer, but maybe your mom does. Can you ask her?" Big brown eyes blinked back at me as the student said, "I did ask my mom, she told me to ask my teacher." I answered the rest of her questions in the same manner. Another

Difficult Questions	Honest Answers
What does death mean?	Death means that the body stops working. Sometimes people die when they are very old, very ill, or so injured that doctors and nurses can't make their bodies work anymore. Your friend is dead and will not be alive again. It is sad.
Was it my fault?	Definitely not. You did not cause this to happen and it is in no way your fault. Sometimes kids can have guilty thoughts. They think if a person died or left, it must be their fault. That is not true and that is not what happened here.
My sister is dying, what can I do?	It is very sad to think of your sister dying. She is with you now and there are things you can do to make her feel better. You can make her food, you can give her medicine, you can tell her a favorite story or a funny joke. You can even quietly hold her hand. That can be very comforting if she feels ill or tired.
Will I die too?	That is a good question. I think you will live a long time, but no one can promise when or where someone will die. Lots of children worry about their health after someone they know dies.
What if I forget about my mom?	It is scary to think about forgetting your mom. We can do things to help you remember her. It is common for children like you to think if they aren't thinking about their person all the time it means they have forgotten them or don't love them. You don't have to think about your mom all the time to love her. It's okay.

student chimed in, asking if you caught cancer like you would catch a cold. Then another student asked if pneumonia would kill her dad.

This discussion did take up some class time, but was worth it. Maybe you, like me, have read books about teaching that advise

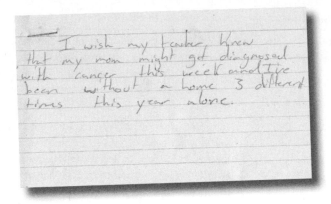

I wish my teacher knew that my mom might get diagnosed with cancer this week and I've been without a home 3 different times this year alone.

you not to allow your class to get side-tracked and keep a laser focus on the lesson at hand, but I think about this little girl wondering all day if her grandmother was going to die. Had I not addressed her concern, she would not have been able to do any of the rigorous work I expected of her with this burning question racing around in her mind. For me, these discussions are not a distraction but rather a key to allow for learning. By being open with my students, I am able to create a sense of community and an environment where all students can have their concerns addressed, so they can turn their attention to learning.

If your students lead you into a discussion like this, remember that you can always say, "I don't know the answer to that. Maybe someone else does, we can ask." Ending your conversations by saying, "If you think of any other questions, let me know" helps a child know their questions and concerns are valid and they can come to you. They may come to you with more questions or they may not, but feeling that there is a person who cares about them and is willing to answer their questions eases a grieving child's anxiety and frees up mental space for learning.

These are difficult conversations, but resist the urge to avoid them. The National Alliance for Grieving Children explains that "although it may be challenging to share the truth about how someone died, honest answers build trust, help provide understanding and allow children to feel comfortable approaching us with questions because they know they can trust us to tell them the truth. Children know more than we think they do and by not telling the truth, we risk leaving children to process complicated information on their own, rather than with the loving adults in their lives."

When a child experiences a loss, their emotional and physical stability can be disrupted, but as they ask questions and get honest answers, they are able to process and understand a tragic event.

2. Memory Books

Memory Books are a way for a grieving child to record their feelings, thoughts, and memories of a person who is not with them. How you choose to put together a Memory Book is very flexible. It can take the form of a written journal, a photo album, or even a shoebox of special objects. Some cultures' form of a Memory Book is a small table or altar in the home or workplace dedicated to the remembrance of a loved one. A Memory Book can be completed by an individual child or, when a loss affects a whole class, compiled by a group of students.

The Memory Book functions as a way for students to find a home for their ruminating thoughts of a person who has died or is not able to be present. This work is helpful in the same way that a to-do list aids us in assembling and categorizing tasks that need to be completed. Instead of obsessing over all the things that need to be done so we don't forget them, simply processing those ideas and recording them allows us to focus on completing tasks and activities. For a grieving child, recording their memories provides comfort that their memories will not be lost and gives them mental permission to contemplate other things.

You might consider including the following within a Memory Book:

- Photos or drawings of the special person
- The special person's biographical information, including their birthday and the day they died
- How the person died
- Favorite memories, funny memories, sad memories
- Interviews that record memories of friends and family
- How the child wishes things could be
- A letter to their special person or what they wish they could tell their special person
- How the other members of the child's family are grieving
- What life was like before and what life is like now
- What feelings the child has experienced
- A list of what the child is worried about
- A list of hopes the child has
- What it was like at the funeral or the last time they saw the person
- A list of allies a child can talk to when they need support

These can be acutely personal topics to discuss, but they are all thoughts a bereaved child is likely contemplating. Teachers can use good judgment and sensitivity in the creation of a Memory Book that provides a safe way for a child to open up about their experiences. While compiling their Memory Book, students are able to discuss the grief incident and what thoughts or questions they might have. If those thoughts stay locked in the child's head, they become difficult to process. Creating some form of Memory Book allows a grieving child to relive their experiences and process those memories while feeling secure and heard.

3. Grief Rituals

Most of us who have experienced a loss have performed a grief ritual to help us process the death or loss of a person we cared about. We may have lit a candle, said a prayer, or participated in a moment of silence. We do these rituals for a reason: they help console us and work through feelings of sorrow and abandonment in productive ways.

Grief rituals can be thought of as deliberate gestures of remembrance that hold a significant meaning to participants. Your school might even have evidence of a grief ritual; our school does. We have a flower garden and a carefully painted rocking chair that commemorate the memory of a student who passed away. Teachers can take an active role in creating and allowing for grief rituals after a loss is experienced.

Often when there is an incident that impacts a school community, school districts have a plan or recommendations in place. Your school district may have some form of a crisis response team that can assist with ideas and making arrangements for a grief ritual as part of their action plan. It might be meaningful for students or community members to participate in the planning of an event or ritual.

Grief Rituals in Schools

- Release balloons
- Hold moments of silence
- Hold a community forum for families, parents, staff members, and students
- Name a community space, like a gymnasium, auditorium, or field
- Produce a memory video
- Compose songs, poems, or raps
- Display photographs publicly
- Make a mailbox available for students to "send" letters
- Create a digital memorial on social media
- Host a memorial event such as a talent show, spelling bee, sports game
- Read a piece of literature, as a community, on a related topic

Some of these rituals might feel difficult to participate in, especially if an incident has impacted you personally. One of the most powerful things we can do for our students in a time of loss is to model our own grief. As stable and caring adults we can demonstrate a positive, empathetic response to a significant loss that our students will pay attention to. Being open and authentic with our feelings helps create an atmosphere where students feel free to share their thoughts and feelings too.

Some deaths, especially those that can be viewed as preventable, can carry an extra weight. The Dougy Center, a national center for grieving children and families, recommends that all deaths and losses in a school community be acknowledged in the same way, whether it is a tragic accident, a drug- or alcohol-impacted death, or a suicide. They "believe very strongly that whatever policy or precedent the school sets should apply to all deaths" because "not having the same activity you would provide in a different kind of death gives the message that the student's life was not valued, or that we should sweep suicide deaths under the rug." According to the Dougy Center, memorials for a student who has died as a result of suicide do not encourage others to take their lives. Rather, it is "an excellent opportunity to educate your students, staff and school community about preventing suicide."

Still, not all grief rituals need to be community focused or public. Private grief rituals can provide comfort as well. These rituals are often unique and deeply personal, like taking special care in packing up the possessions left behind, cataloguing photos of the loved one, or cherishing gifts given.

When I was a sophomore in high school my older sister left home for the first time and moved to Quito, Ecuador. On the surface I was unaffected. I did not want my family or teachers to know how much I missed her, for fear they would think I was overly sensitive. Secretly, I slipped into her bedroom each night and slept in her daybed for weeks after she left, carefully making the bed each morning so as to not be detected. While this loss certainly was not as acute as a death, I realize that I was doing this in order to ease the pain of my sister's absence. It was my form of a private grief ritual.

Teachers do not necessarily need to provide private grief rituals for students, but we should accommodate them. A bereaved student might benefit from fidgeting with a special necklace, looking at photos on their cell phone, or listening to music that holds a special significance. Sometimes students experiencing grief feel comforted and protected by something as simple as baggy clothing or large jackets, which provide physical comfort as well as a psychological protective barrier. Exceptions to school rules might need to be made in order to allow for these private grief rituals.

The presence of grief rituals throughout time and across cultures speaks to their significance in the mourning process. As educators, we should become more comfortable taking an active role in providing and allowing for these experiences for our students. In this way we provide healing.

4. Legacy Projects: Looking Back, Giving Forward

After a loss grieving students often feel powerless. They feel as though they have no control over what has happened. The feelings of helplessness can be overwhelming. One way to overcome this is to lead your students in carrying out a Legacy Project, a service project that helps them feel empowered to take action on a related topic. There are a multitude of ways a Legacy Project can come to fruition. For bereaved students, participating in an activity uniquely connected to the person who was lost or taking active steps to raise awareness and contribute to prevention can be healing.

There is no need to rush into implementing a Legacy Project. It is completely fine to take time, even a substantial amount of time, to deal with the loss and meet the community's initial needs. Similarly, there is no wrong or right way to approach a Legacy Project. However, keep in mind that the goal is to

Legacy Projects

- Plant a memorial garden or tree
- Send cards to surviving family members or friends
- Create an art installation like a mural or mosaic
- Raise funds to donate to a connected charity
- Create an informational poster or website on a related topic
- Raise awareness through a social media campaign
- Research a related topic and interview experts in the field in order to compose books or essays that share findings
- Write newspaper articles or op-ed pieces taking a stance on a related topic
- Donate books or toys to a related charity
- Teach younger children a lesson on a related topic
- Take care of the family's home as they grieve
- Plan a community meal or activity with a special meaning

empower your students to take action and by doing so regain a sense of control as they search for meaning in a loss.

Make sure students or the school community are truly in charge of the project and that you, as the teacher, take on the role of facilitator. A Legacy Project should be open to anyone who wants to participate, but the project should also be optional, so those who choose to process the loss in their own way have the space to do so.

Additionally, Legacy Projects should be done in partnership with grieving family members and loved ones. I know a family whose daughter suddenly and tragically passed away during the school year. In response, the school created a loving memorial

In My Classroom

Tara Seekins, Asst. Head of School, Willow Creek Academy

What strikes me, all these years later, was the timing of it all. My fourth-grade class had just read *Sadako and the Thousand Paper Cranes* by Eleanor Coerr, a novel based on the true story of a girl who developed cancer as a result of radiation in her hometown of Hiroshima, Japan. In the book, Sadako consoles herself by making origami cranes. If she can reach her goal of making one thousand origami cranes, her best friend tells her, she will be rewarded with one wish.

Just as we finished the story, the mother of one of my students came up to me and explained that her son Bruno, perfectly healthy days ago, had collapsed over the weekend. Soon we found out it was the result of a brain tumor. Bruno would undergo radiation therapy and would not be returning to our school.

At first, I struggled to make sense of it all, but I resolved to do everything in my power to nurture Bruno and support his thirty-three classmates through this time of unimaginable grief. My first step was to make myself available to Bruno's family. I would be his home-hospital teacher and would keep Bruno in contact with his classmates. Then, I had the wearying task of presenting the awful news to the class. The discussion was difficult and painful. It was hard, but I was honest and direct. I allowed their concerns and curiosity to drive the conversation. I found myself answering questions like "Why did Bruno get cancer?" and "Can I catch it?" I followed up our discussion with a note home to the families in our classroom and made myself available for their questions too.

Very shortly after learning of his condition, Bruno's classmates devised a plan to fold one thousand origami paper cranes, in the spirit of Sadako, in hopes that it would grant them one precious wish. So, colorful paper began to be folded and creased by a collection of little fingers. Over the next weeks, my industrious students kept track of their progress towards their goal on the board in thick blue marker: first "943 cranes to go" then "662 cranes to go." A few children even opened up a "Crane Hospital" where they fixed up any frail cranes in need of care, just like their friend. Soon there were "456 cranes to go" and "125 cranes to go" and finally just one crane to go. The honor of folding the final paper crane was given to Bruno's best friend, who triumphantly strung up the last paper creation to the strand.

The moment had come to make our hard-earned wish. Even now, ten years later, the image of Bruno's thirty-three classmates sitting cross-legged in total concentration is still with me. With their fists clenched and eyes scrunched, each student focusing every ounce of energy on a singular expression of hope for their friend's survival. It remains the most potent assertion of humanity I have ever experienced.

Once again, the timing of it all caught me off guard. Just as I attempted to arrange a classroom visit, Bruno's mother called to inform me that Bruno had taken a turn for the worse. His health was deteriorating very quickly. He would not be able to do any more schooling and visiting the school was now unfeasible. I was heartbroken. I too had grasped on to his classmates' sincere belief in the healing power of paper cranes.

Desperate to preserve the wish, I rushed to the hospital with a rainbow of paper cranes in the backseat of my car. Under a wobbling heap of folded paper, I summoned all my courage and tottered into the pediatric intensive care unit, then lovingly draped exactly one thousand paper cranes onto Bruno's IV tower.

The reality of his circumstance was apparent. Bruno was no longer the energetic child he had been just months ago. His body strained as he turned to take in the paper waterfall that hung haphazardly beside him. As the corners of a smile spread across his

continues

continued

swollen cheeks, a sense of comfort came over me as I realized that Bruno understood the significance of every last paper crane.

Our work was not in vain. This was powerful medicine.

In the end, Bruno's fate was the same as Sadako's. He passed away a few months after the cranes and the wish were delivered. As a class, we created a memorial space outside of our classroom where we hung a plaque engraved with a paper crane and dedicated the space to his memory.

I wouldn't wish this experience upon any child, any teacher, or any classroom. Coping with this loss was more than the beautiful act of forming paper cranes. It was also incredibly painful. As a young teacher with limited personal experience with loss of this magnitude, I could not have planned or prepared for the toll such a tragedy would take.

Bruno's body did not deserve the suffering it was put through. But he did deserve to know just how much his classmates cared about him. I know that it was my responsibility to shepherd my students through the loss of their friend. It was also my opportunity to be the teacher my students needed. Through this sorrowful circumstance, I was challenged to access empathy and inner resources I never knew existed, and the same can be said for Bruno's classmates.

I want teachers to know tragedy may happen in your classroom. If it does, embrace it as an opportunity to come to your work with more heart than you ever thought was imaginable, to model healthy heartbreak, and be a source of strength during the healing.

by dedicating a bench in her name. The bench unintendedly caused some mixed feelings for the girl's younger brother who continued attending the school. The family wanted teachers to know that "it is important to consider the impact a project or memorial may have on other siblings still attending the school, especially, if it is a permanent fixture. We were touched by the gesture, but would have loved to be included in the discussions."

When the larger community is witness to acts of service through a Legacy Project, it is an impressive model of generosity and empowerment. At our school, we have such a model. Without fail, on the very first day of school one of my ardent new students will ask the question, "When is Alyssa coming?" Alyssa never attended our school. My class and I never had the pleasure of meeting Alyssa, yet, her presence has blessed our school community.

The Alyssa the children speak of is Alyssa Hemmelgarn, a fourth-grade girl whose compassion and love of reading characterized her life. Alyssa passed away on March 8, 2007, only ten short days after being diagnosed with leukemia. In commemoration of her love of books, the organization Alyssa Cares was created. Her parents, Joe and Carole Hemmelgarn, visit five elementary schools in Denver several times a year to tell Alyssa's story and put brand new books in the hands and homes of each student. To date, more than fifty thousand books have been cherished by students thanks to her legacy.

Through Alyssa Cares, my students are able to select a new book to take home, but they receive a much greater gift. Each time Joe and Carole come to our school they tell our students about a book Alyssa loved as well as share her story. "Giving books to children is a gift to us," explains Carole. "We have the opportunity to talk about our daughter and kids are able to ask questions." For me, this has created an opportunity to discuss death and grief in an authentic way in my classroom. Just as important as giving books is providing students with a positive grief model.

A Legacy Project you facilitate does not have to be as involved as forming a nonprofit organization, however, Joe and Carole's example shows the ripple effect of a Legacy Project. As Carole says, "Our hope is that children, even young children, nurture the love of reading like our daughter, but we also want them to see the impact that one person can make." Not only can you and your students take active steps to process a loss and make a positive impact on the community in the process, but you can also be a model for your wider community.

5. Grief and Loss Inventory

Since we know loss impacts a critical mass of our students and issues of grief may manifest themselves long after an incident occurs, one step a school can take is to create and maintain a Grief and Loss Inventory. The goal of a schoolwide Grief and Loss Inventory is to make the appropriate teachers and school staff aware of what a particular student is coping with so they can be empathetic and supportive. Professor Linda Goldman describes a Grief and Loss Inventory as "a tool for creating and storing history on the grieving child throughout his or her academic life."

To respect our students' privacy, this can be done with permission from families and the impacted students themselves. Often, families and students are appreciative of having this information shared, albeit in caring ways, so there is widespread

Example of Grief and Loss Inventory
_____

Student Name:

Brief explanation of grief incident:

Family members and friends affected:

Important dates to be aware of:

Observations prior to grief incident:

Known challenges:

Successful interventions:

Less successful interventions:

Further notes:

_____

understanding and support without the need to individually retell their story to each teacher or staff member. It might also be appropriate to provide the family and sometimes the student with a copy of their entry in the school's Grief and Loss Inventory, so they are informed and approve of all information being shared.

When a school community compiles an inventory, it is helpful to collect general information on the grief incident itself; it is also important to include relevant dates such as birthdays and deaths of loved ones that may have a great impact on the child through the years. A thoughtful teacher might include notes on activities or topics that might be difficult for the student to explore as a result of their grief. Information on what could send a student into an agitated state as well as which interventions have been beneficial and which have not will ultimately help the child's future teachers and other school staff support the student.

If the grief incident occurred in the middle of the student's academic career, it can be very helpful for an educator to record information and observations about the student's behaviors and academic process prior to the event occurring. Grief can manifest in ways that look similar to symptoms of learning disabilities and attention disorders, which means this information can be helpful to teachers and families so they are better able to differentiate true learning disabilities from grief-related behavior.

Imagine a student who lost his father when he was five years old. Certainly his kindergarten teacher would know of this, and his first-grade teacher might also have been made aware of the situation. However, without a systematic way of preserving this information, the likelihood of each successive year's teacher understanding the impact of his circumstances drops. Imagine now, that same little boy in sixth grade getting into a physical fight on the anniversary of his father's death.

A thoughtful educator made aware of how grief has affected this boy would be more likely to connect the dots and see the fight as related to feelings of loss than a teacher who has no knowledge of the student's history. The informed teacher would certainly take action to ameliorate the harm caused by the fight, but he or she would also be able to support the student by addressing the root cause of the incident. If knowledge of the student's grief and loss had not been preserved in a school-wide inventory, educators and administrators could not have a complete understanding of the incident. A Grief and Loss Inventory helps us record information that might otherwise be overlooked so we can support our students in the best way possible.

You might feel that you do not have enough expertise or training to support a grieving child. But feel encouraged that as a teacher you do not need to be an expert in grief and loss to make a positive impact during a difficult situation. You are a caring adult and can be present and authentic. Do not underestimate the impact of this. As Professor Goldman writes in her book *Children Also Grieve,* "We are powerless to control the losses and catastrophic events our children may need to face. But by honoring their inner wisdom, providing mentorship, and creating safe havens for expression, we can empower them to become more capable and more caring human beings."

he broke my heart when
she declared that my
art isn't good enough.

that it was difficult to pay attention
in class, not knowing where I was
going to sleep at night

WISH MU
eacher
new
ve m
famil

I wish my teacher knew that
I've lived a hard life and I try
my hardest and best to remark

wish my t
at my mom a
a argument e
effect me a
hen they do
led and my

I wish my teachers know that I am
not the happy person they see every
morning. I wish my teachers knew
that I tried attempting to end my
life multiple times but came to
school right after. I wish my teachers
knew that I am drowning in a
sea of sorrow and they keep throwing
anchors instead of life preservers.

knew th
to a chi

my mom might get diagnos
with cancer this week and I
been without a home 3 dif
times this year alone.

wish my teacher knew
at moving schools its
rd to make friends
th people you feel don't
e you.

I wish my teacher knew that
I hated to go back to the cho
y night & it was difficult to
attention in class

wish my teacher knew that
metimes my feelings and
otions are already crushed when
walk into class and he/she
akes it worse by being hosti

I WISH
teacher
knew I
love back

o not pressure kids when they
on't even whats going on at
ome.

5.

When Students Are in Danger
Supporting Students in the Trauma-Informed Classroom

My Classroom Community

A week before our school year ended, my class was putting together a book of all the stories, jokes, and learning that had happened that year. One student was writing down her favorite song of the school year, which sparked a conversation with her tablemate. I didn't hear the beginning of their conversation, but from the corner of our classroom I heard one girl make a comment that shook me. "Yeah, he beat Rihanna up, but you know it was her fault. She deserved it."

They were talking about the tragic incident of recording artist Chris Brown assaulting his then-girlfriend Rihanna, another famous singer. The incident had been all over the news and trickled down to the students in my classroom. There wasn't much ambiguity to the facts of the case: Chris Brown was under investigation for felony battery, and photos of Rihanna's bruised face had been leaked to the press. It was pretty easy for anyone to connect the dots, but it seemed that some of the young minds in my room had only partially understood the situation. Even more troubling was that some had come to the conclusion that the innocent woman had brought the abuse on herself.

This comment, which my student made so casually, upset me. Had she overhead this statement and was repeating it? Or was this her own conclusion? Perhaps she was led to believe women are at fault more often than men because of a larger cultural narrative, or perhaps she simply was at the point in her life when kids believe bad things only happen to bad people. Either way, I felt it was my responsibility as a teacher and as a caring adult to address her comment.

Abuse was an intimidating subject for me to approach as a teacher. I could have ignored her comment or quickly told her to not say something like that, but instead I explored her thoughts further. I asked her, "What do you mean? Tell me more about that." She explained that she didn't know much about the case but had heard her family talking about it. Murmurings and whispers swept through the room, and numerous students raised their hands, eager to share their personal experiences.

I remember the conversation clearly. One student explained how he had used his small body to hold the bathroom door shut in order to protect himself and his little sister from the rage of his mother's ex-boyfriend. Another student shared the story of the time his intoxicated father threw the TV across their room, forcing the child and his mother to flee barefoot in the snow to safety in a neighbor's apartment. One child told how his father had heroically intervened in a physical fight to protect a family friend. And another explained that the reason her cousins now lived with her family was because they had gotten hit before. Yet another child told of a bloody handprint left on the wall of their new apartment. "I can still see it in my mind," he said

Adverse Childhood Experiences in America

Below are a few of the startling statistics that demonstrate the realities of abuse in America:

- In 2013, forty-seven states reported approximately 3.1 million children received preventative services from Child Protective Services agencies in the United States.
- Of the children who experienced maltreatment or abuse, nearly 80 percent suffered neglect; 18 percent suffered physical abuse; and 9 percent suffered sexual abuse.
- One in fifteen children is exposed to intimate partner violence each year, and 90 percent of these children are eyewitnesses to the violence.
- About one in ten children will be sexually abused before they turn eighteen years old.

Knowing the reality of abuse in America is the first step to becoming a trauma-informed educator. The National Coalition Against Domestic Violence encourages "local schools and youth programs to train teachers, school counselors, and athletic coaches on how to recognize children and teens who are victims of intimate partner violence. Provide educators with resources and prepare them to intervene in domestic violence, dating violence, and stalking situations."

flatly. For me, it was shocking to realize this topic elicited such a strong outpouring of emotions and that so many of my students had such personal experiences of abuse.

But I was most taken aback by Sonny's story. He told the class something quite shocking. Sonny had just arrived at our

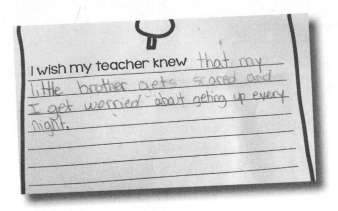

I wish my teacher knew that my little brother gets scared and I get worried about geting up every night.

school. He had come from a Mexican city on the border. He told the story of his journey to America, and the incident that caused his mother and himself to flee for their lives.

He told us all how his father would fight with his mother, but because his father was "friends with the president," as he put it in his developing English, his father never got in trouble. Sonny told me of the day he and his mother escaped. He had to run from the door of his house to the car while his father was shooting a gun at his mother. As Sonny told the class his story, his big brown eyes looked up at me and a broad forced smile kept his tears at bay. I marveled at how such a little boy had been so strong.

Abuse in America

While most of my students have not experienced abuse, the hard truth I learned that afternoon is that some have. Looking at the statistics, I know that some of the students in my classroom are likely experiencing abuse or coping with the fallout every day but not telling anyone. The statistics on how many of America's children experience abuse show an appalling reality. As teachers, we want to believe the children in our classrooms are the exception, that our students are the lucky few who defy the statistics, and that this is an issue for other people's classrooms.

But we are most likely wrong.

A study published in *JAMA Pediatrics* in 2014 found that 5 percent of American children experienced abuse. That number is based on cases confirmed by Child Protective Services between 2004 and 2011. But the study's researchers made sure to point out that the actual number of children mistreated at some point before the age of eighteen was probably much larger. Approximately one in eight children will experience some form of abuse or neglect in their own home.

Based on sheer statistics, every teacher is extremely likely to encounter students within their classroom who have lived through adverse childhood experiences. We must be prepared to listen and act effectively when that situation arises.

The Trauma-Informed Teacher

Teachers can best serve their students when they educate through a trauma-informed lens. According to the Trauma-Informed Care Project, "Becoming trauma-informed means recognizing that people often have many different types of trauma in their lives. People who have been traumatized need support and understanding from those around them." Loss of safety is a defining characteristic of trauma. When a student does not feel safe, they are unable to access the parts of the brain that control higher-level thinking, including the ability to learn.

An emphasis on acting as a trauma-informed educator is to minimize the effects of trauma in the learning environment; we

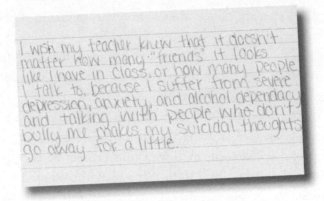

I wish my teacher knew that it doesn't matter how many "friends" it looks like I have in class, or how many people I talk to, because I suffer from severe depression, anxiety, and alcohol dependacy and talking with people who don't bully me makes my suicidal thoughts go away for a little.

can do this by not allowing our words or actions to retraumatize students and by supporting these students in the classroom. "Trauma is an overwhelming event, it takes away our safety, it creates a sense of helplessness, and it continues to affect our perception of our reality," explains Dr. James Henry, director of the Children's Trauma Assessment Center. "For these students danger is right around the corner. The brain gets wired to expect danger."

Trauma-informed practices are not always intensive individual interventions. Teachers don't need to wait for special permission or district mandates; we can create supports for our entire class. "My first step was establishing the Safe Place," explains Jodi Grove, a teacher at Edison Elementary in Walla Walla, Washington:

It was simply a space behind my desk where my first-grade students could go to deescalate in a safe manner. By going into the Safe Place, it signaled to me as the teacher that a particular student needed support, that he or she needed to feel safe and have his or her feelings acknowledged. When a student is able to return to a calm and regulated state, they are usually able to tell me what triggered such a strong reaction. The incident could have been instigated by something as small as not getting the color crayon they wanted. After a short discussion, even the child knows it had nothing to do with the crayon. I have found that six-year-olds are surprisingly capable of identifying the source of their trauma or loss. Because of the Safe Place, one student was able to tell me he was confused and angry because his dad just left. Another let me know how acutely she feels the absence of her mother who is incarcerated.

Before I implemented the Safe Place, my only recourse was to send students to their seats with their heads down. Now, I have seen firsthand, students who are in an escalated state go straight to the Safe Place and use strategies to calm their bodies. I knew that the change was working when one of my students went to music class and asked the teacher where the Safe Place was in her room. By making a deliberate effort to become a trauma-informed teacher I have learned that my students need love, so much love. But, they also need an empathetic teacher who can teach them how to self-regulate in a safe manner so they can learn.

Feel encouraged that there are probably already a multitude of strategies you are using in your classroom right now that are supportive of students dealing with trauma. For instance, providing predictable rituals and routines, being steady and consistent in your tone, or simply regularly checking in with students you are concerned about are all immensely helpful. A teacher's job is to respond to the varied needs of all students, and we have an ethical imperative to respond to those in crisis with love and to the letter of the law.

Trauma and the Law

I am a mandatory reporter. The Child Welfare Information Gateway offers a wealth of information on mandatory reporting laws. They describe a mandatory reporter as a person "required to report suspected child maltreatment to an appropriate agency, such as child protective services, a law enforcement agency, or a State's toll-free child abuse reporting hotline." Requirements for mandatory reporting vary from state to state. "Typically, a report must be made when the reporter, in his or her official capacity, suspects or has reason to believe that a child has been abused or neglected. Another standard frequently used is in situations in which the reporter has knowledge of, or observes a child being subjected to conditions that would reasonably result in harm to the child."

This means there are many people who are not only empowered to report child abuse and neglect, but also legally required to do so. Exactly who is a mandatory reporter varies by state, but in forty-eight states mandatory reporters include teachers, principals, and other school personnel. Safe Horizon, an organization that works to provide support, prevent violence, and promote justice for victims of abuse, states that 17 percent of all reports of child abuse and neglect are made by teachers. As educators we are also in the company of medical workers, social workers, law enforcement officers, and mental health professionals as mandatory reporters. Some states also include clergy, athletic staff, and animal control officers as legally required reporters of abuse or neglect. In all, there is a massive network of adults who are mandatory reporters. However, I would like the entire nation to join the eighteen states that legally require any person who suspects child abuse or neglect to report their concerns.

As a teacher I know it is my legal responsibility to report child abuse or neglect. I do not see this as a burden, but as my duty to do everything I can to ensure the safety and well-being of the children I am trusted with during the school day. Like almost every teacher I know, I have indeed officially reported my concerns of child abuse.

The sad reality is that I have felt the need to make reports every single year I have been teaching. The first few times, I was especially anxious to report my concerns about abuse and neglect to state agencies. I felt the weight of responsibility to help the children whom I suspected were suffering abuse. I have also felt discouraged and let down when my concerns were not followed up by our state child welfare agency.

There is no official notification to the implicated party as to who actually reports concerns, yet sometimes the suspected abuser has connected the report back to me. I have been confronted by a parent I implicated in a report. While this particular situation did not turn violent, I have seen a confrontation between a suspected abuser and school personnel turn into a threatening encounter. In this situation our school followed guidelines provided by our school district's safety and security department. I encourage educators to familiarize themselves with the procedures and resources their school districts offer.

Personally, I feel the need to do more than just report my concerns. As a teacher I feel compelled to advocate for all American children who experience abuse and neglect. I believe we teachers can all be voices for change in our communities. We can speak truth to decision-makers about the need for adequate funding and trained personnel to respond to our concerns of abuse. We can speak up for more comprehensive programs that support our students who have been traumatized. We can seek more information about how trauma is affecting

Know the Signs of Abuse

Abuse and trauma can manifest differently in different children, sometimes leading to guilt, shame, and confusion. Due to the complex nature of abuse, children do not often make explicit cries for help. The Department of Justice advises, "A common presumption is that children will give one detailed, clear account of abuse. This is not consistent with research; disclosures often unfold gradually and may be presented in a series of hints." Because of this, it is vital that educators are aware of red flags and warning signs so we can respond appropriately.

The Mayo Clinic provides an extensive list (below) of symptoms of abuse and neglect, but also cautions us "keep in mind that warning signs are just that: warning signs. The presence of warning signs doesn't necessarily mean a child is being abused." The clinic emphasizes that when abuse or neglect is suspected, the concerned party should contact the appropriate agencies or departments.

Physical abuse signs and symptoms
- Unexplained injuries, such as bruises, fractures, or burns
- Injuries that don't match the given explanation
- Untreated medical or dental problems

Sexual abuse signs and symptoms
- Sexual behavior or knowledge that's inappropriate for the child's age
- Pregnancy or a sexually transmitted infection
- Statements that he or she was sexually abused

- Trouble walking or sitting or complaints of genital pain
- Abuse of other children sexually

Emotional abuse signs and symptoms

- Delayed or inappropriate emotional development
- Loss of self-confidence or self-esteem
- Social withdrawal or a loss of interest or enthusiasm
- Depression
- Headaches or stomachaches with no medical cause
- Avoidance of certain situations, such as refusing to go to school or ride the bus
- Desperately seeking affection
- A decrease in school performance or loss of interest in school
- Loss of previously acquired developmental skills

Neglect signs and symptoms

- Poor growth or weight gain
- Poor hygiene
- Lack of clothing or supplies to meet physical needs
- Taking food or money without permission
- Eating a lot in one sitting or hiding food for later
- Poor record of school attendance
- Lack of appropriate attention for medical, dental, or psychological problems or lack of necessary follow-up care
- Emotional swings that are inappropriate or out of context to the situation
- Indifference

our classrooms and demand training to develop our abilities to support students who are suffering. Teachers especially have the power to make a difference on this issue.

Teacher Tools

1. Identify Your Allies

While many of my students will never struggle with abuse, self-harm, or emotional challenges, I know some will. Yet it's impossible to predict exactly which students these will be. I often have meetings about these topics with my whole class, casting a wide net and hoping to catch the students who need catching. Inspired by Signs of Suicide, an evidence-based suicide prevention intervention program, aimed at adolescents, one purpose of these conversations is to have students identify exactly which people in their lives could be allies if a difficult situation were to arise.

The term "ally" is so appropriate. "Teacher" does not fully encompass our role in our students' lives. What then? Friend? Certainly we should be friendly to our students, but teachers who put themselves in the position of friend do a disservice to their role in their students' lives.

Wendy O. Osefo, professor and graduate director at Goucher College, says this:

Allyship is a much deeper bond and relationship than just the average teacher-to-student. As an ally you not only provide guidance to the student, you also provide a voice for the student. With allyship, teachers both empower and support students. Most importantly, students feel as though they have a partner in the educational process. This relationship is also a benefit to teachers. Students are more keen to listen and take risks as learners due to the underlying trust and relationship the allyship has created. Furthermore, in times of hardship, a teacher will act as an ally by walking through all the steps with the student—from reporting the incident to recovery. As an ally, a teacher will not simply "hand the student off" to the counselor, but rather walk them through the entire process while providing both an ear and shoulder if needed.

As allies, the image of walking through a time of hardship with our students is powerful. Just having someone to walk beside them can change realities for a student. Numerous studies have shown the benefits allies and mentors can have. A study from Brigham Young University found that "for all teen students, having an adult mentor meant a 50 percent greater likelihood of attending college. For disadvantaged students, mentorship by a teacher nearly doubled the odds of attending college."

Whatever the challenge may be, whether it is overwhelming or just the expected struggle of growing up, students need to know there are people who can support them. Some students might already know exactly who to turn to when they need help because they have a close-knit support system, but others will need help identifying their allies. In particular, students who have encountered abuse are going to be especially unclear about whom they can turn to, since often the abuse has occurred at the hands of a trusted adult.

Start the conversation by discussing what an ally is. Talk about where students have heard this term before, or have them look up its definition. Then discuss what it means to have an ally and why allies are important. Help students identify the allies they have in their lives. They might initially think of peers,

In My Classroom
Sara Bradbury, Director

Sara Bradbury works at Hope Academy of the Denver Street School, a school for girls who have been victims of domestic sex trafficking or sexual exploitation. To honor her students' experiences and privacy, she speaks of her students as an amalgamation.

I'm not your normal teacher. Everything I do in our classes is centered around supporting an amazing group of girls who have been through incredibly traumatic experiences. But, the thing is, if you think our students are unique, you are wrong. Each and every one of my students was in a normal general education classroom when the abuse perpetrated on them began. They had normal homework, normal recess, and, yes, normal teachers.

The truth is, there was an opportunity for normal teachers to intervene in the early stages of abuse for each one of our students. In looking at academic records, it was documented that a student was showing signs of extreme exhaustion in

their friends, or siblings, which is common. Ultimately, you want students to identify adults as their allies as well. If a student goes to another child with a significant problem, the child might not have the ability to help, or it might be too much to for them to handle. It is okay to tell children this.

Then lead students in brainstorming which adults are their allies both in school and outside of school. Have them write down their list of allies. Simply writing down names can make class years before there was any contact made to social services or the police reported a concern. If her teachers had been able to see this exhaustion not as laziness or inattention but as it truly was—a warning sign of the abuse she was suffering—maybe this girl could have gotten support much sooner.

There are several other warning signs that teachers should be aware of. Some of the most common I have seen are students having a sudden and unexplained access to money or expensive gifts, a sudden and dramatic change in academic performance, or isolation from their peers or family. In my experience, a student who has suffered sexual abuse can present a wide range of emotional reactions, from muting their emotions to extreme reactions of anger and sadness.

I wish that there were more cases when caring adults acted on their concerns and reached out to support services sooner. I want teachers to know that abuse and human trafficking are not issues for other people's classrooms. Each teacher is in a situation to intervene and be a light in their students' lives.

it "official" in their eyes. You may have students who claim they don't have a single ally. That is fine; this activity is made for them. When this happens, I write my name on the board. The next step is very important: explicitly state to your students that you are their ally.

So many times we teachers think this is implied and that their students know they can come to us. Still, make sure you say out loud, "I am your ally. You can trust me." Students can carry this list with them, but by simply having them identify and document their allies, you are giving students a first step to reaching out for help when they need it.

My Allies at School

1.

2.

3.

My Allies Outside of School

1.

2.

3.

What My Teacher Didn't Know
Sophia's Story

Today, I can confidently say I am a strong mother and a dedicated social worker, but as a child my life was anything but peaceful. My mother battled substance abuse for most of my childhood. As a result I was placed in foster care several times. During one of those placements, I was required to see a therapist. It infuriated me. My mother had the problems, not me. Why did I have to sit in that shabby room and be assaulted by questions from some lady who didn't know me at all?

I sat in her office, arms crossed and brow furrowed as she tried to make a crack in my defenses by playing a board game. A few minutes into moving little plastic people around colored squares she told me that I could trust her and she knew where I was coming from. I remember that sentence so clearly. "I know where you are coming from," she said.

My reaction was the textbook response. My guard was up as I investigated her statement. "Really?" I said. "Have you ever been beaten by your stepdad as your mother watched, too afraid to help you?" I asked.

"No," she replied sheepishly.

I lit into her with a battery of questions, aiming to hurt her with the truth about my life: "Have you ever been too embarrassed to beg for food so you sat hungry for three days while your mom went out for cigarettes? Have you ever used your Christmas wish to ask Santa for your mom to come back because you think Santa is the only adult in the world who gives children what they want?"

Her reply to my inquisition was a retreating, "No."

I fired my final shot, "Then how could you know where I was coming from?" With that I flipped over the flimsy game board and marched out.

At that point in my life, I could have raised the white flag right there and declared my distrust of adults final. The adults I was exposed to never kept their promises and rarely spoke honestly to me. But, fortunately, as the game board flipped in the air, I made a silent declaration to myself. Someday, I would be a grown-up. I would speak the truth to children. I would be an adult who kept my promises. My life would be dedicated to helping children just like me.

And when I looked in the face of a hurting child and said, "I know where you are coming from," it would be true.

I want teachers to know you don't have to have walked in a child's shoes to support them, but you do need to be honest. Like me, many of your students who have suffered from abuse or neglect cultivate a deep distrust of adults and each well-meaning, but broken, promise builds up their defenses. With the children and families I now serve, I strive to only make promises I can keep.

2. Promises We Can Keep

Sophia's story speaks volumes about the impact our words can have on children when they are in the middle of a crisis. It is so tempting to reassure students and tell them everything will be okay, but that is simply not something we can guarantee. However, there is plenty we can say to children that is both reassuring and true. I encourage teachers to think about true statements they can make to students and have them at the ready.

Promises Teachers Can't Keep	Promises Teachers Can Keep
This won't ever happen to you again.	There are a lot of people who want to help you. I will always care about you.
I can fix this.	I am here to help you. It is my job.
You don't have to worry anymore.	This is not your fault. What has happened to you is not fair and I am sorry you have to deal with this.
I won't let you down.	You don't have to cope with this alone.
It will be okay.	It sounds like there are some really hard things going on that you wish would stop.

3. Regulation Activities

Students who have been exposed to adverse childhood experiences may react differently than others in your classroom. Even long after a traumatic event, children can reexperience fear and terror when sensory input reminds their brain of the previous trauma. For example, a door being slammed, the lights shutting off, or an unexpected touch may seem normal to those of us who have not experienced trauma, but can trigger an intense reaction from children who have. Trauma exposure can cause a student to enter a hypervigilant state in which their body is responding as if there is still an active threat.

When a student is in this heightened state, talking usually doesn't help because they aren't able to think logically. Resist the urge to lecture a student or offer advice. Instead, teachers can respond by offering regulation activities. It is a good idea for the child to practice completing regulation activities before he or she is in a hyperattentive, agitated state so they will know how to do the activity when they need it.

A powerful way to teach self-regulation is simply to model it. The act of teaching can be arduous and frustrating, which presents a great opportunity for teachers to model the self-regulation skills we want to develop in our students. While I am a teacher, I also happen to be a real person who gets frustrated and irritated when I am interrupted. There was a time when my class had not yet developed the self-control to not shout out their thoughts. I kept track of how many times I had to stop and redirect the class; it was forty-two times while reading just twelve pages of a picture book. That's almost once a sentence! I was at my limit and felt overwhelmed and frustrated. So I stopped reading the book and did a breathing exercise.

I often stop my class to calm myself and other times to refocus my students. I might do this three to ten times a day. Really. I say, "I am frustrated and in order to teach you I need to be calm, so I am going to breathe slowly." This signals to the kids that there needs to be a change in behavior and gives them a living example of how to do it for themselves.

Regulation Activities for the Whole Class

Music
Research shows that classical music can help calm students. Upbeat pop music has a similar effect if used thoughtfully. Many popular artists' songs express positive themes such as gratitude, self-appreciation, and kindness. Janessa Malisani, a fifth-grade teacher at my school, uses a new popular song each week to practice fluency, learn figurative language, and discuss how each song's themes relate to her students' lives: "By the end of the week, many of my students are singing the song and dancing in their chairs. It's so great to see the classroom grounded in positivity and joy, while teaching necessary skills."

Breathing Activities
Slow and meditative breathing can help a student regain a sense of calm. Former third-grade teacher Susana Moening introduced the Cortices breathing practice to our school. As a class, we take about forty-five seconds after lunch to breathe slowly as we lightly tap our head and heart. There are so many breathing activities that can be used in a classroom. Find one that works for your students.

Positive Self-Talk
Having a mantra or a class chant can help establish a culture of self-regulation. This can be as simple as "I know I can be calm." When I worked in DC Public Schools, all the students at Stanton Elementary stated, "What my mind can conceive, my heart can believe, I can achieve" each morning during announcements.

Regulation Activities for Individual Students

Bounce-Back Boxes
Offer a small box with calming activities tailored to a specific student's interests. The box may contain clay, stuffed animals, or coloring materials.

For older students this might be headphones for listening to music or even handheld electronics. For some students I include an egg timer so they can monitor how much time it takes them to "bounce back." Remember, it may take more time than you think for a student to regain a calm state of mind.

Safe Place
As in Jodi Grove's classroom, a safe place should be established beforehand. Students need to know where to go, what will happen there, and that they will not be in danger. These spots can be established in individual classrooms or can be a single space available to the whole school.

Video Games
Yes, video games! Once, a child in my classroom had an intense reaction to his father being deported. This caused him to enter a dysfunctional state several times a day. One day, he even attempted to jump out of a second-story window. While our school worked to support him through this time, we found that allowing him to play a simple race car game on a computer brought him to a calmer, more rational state of mind where he could feel safe and be helped.

When a child is in an agitated state, a simple video game can be a perfect way to have them shift their focus from a trauma-triggered hypervigilant state to a calming activity. Simple games like Pac-Man or Tetris are engaging, but don't demand a ton of cognition or attention.

---

4. Take Care of Thyself

If there were commandments for teaching, the very first etched in stone should be "Take care of thyself." Oh, what a difficult commandment this is to follow. I still struggle with it. Most of my evaluation and feedback conversations end with my caring principal urging me to "Take more time for yourself. We don't want you to burn out."

If we are going to help our students through challenging times, we must make sure we are working to resolve our own issues as well. We all have experiences and feelings we need to work through, confidences we need to build, stresses we need to release, and interpersonal conflicts we need to manage.

Dealing with what our students share with us has an effect on us. A while back, a fellow Denver teacher asked me how I deal with the difficult realities I learn about my students' lives. How do I manage knowing about tragedies and traumas children should never have to experience?

He said his high school students completed an exercise similar to "I wish my teacher knew." He helped his students compose personal memoirs that told stories of significant moments in their lives. From this one assignment, four of his students were brave enough to confess they had been sexually assaulted.

As teachers, we wonder if we can possibly support our students through the challenges and problems they face. How can we even bear to hear about all the heartache in our classrooms? I confess I do not have a complete answer to this. I too feel overwhelmed at times by knowing some of the realities my students face.

I go back to a wonderful educator who was my mentor teacher, Rachel Bernard. She told me, "I get the courage to listen and be supportive during the most traumatizing events in my students' lives from the children themselves. If a child is courageous enough to open up to me about what they have experienced, I can be brave enough to listen. My strength comes from their strength, my hope comes from their hope." In the end, I would always rather allow a student to feel heard, even when it hurts to listen.

We can and should take comfort in the fact that by working through our own doubts, insecurities, and traumas we are helping our students do the same for themselves. And we are creating a safe and secure environment in our classrooms.

What would this actually mean? Certainly, teachers need to take responsibility for maintaining their own mental health. But there is also an opportunity for us as educators to create understanding cultures in our schools that are supportive of teachers dealing with some of the same struggles and challenges we want to support our students through.

We can push our school districts and local governments to provide our education professionals with the programs and policies that support their mental and emotional health. It's also important to remember that we can find support from fellow teachers, commiserating and celebrating with others who know the unique realities and responsibilities of our job.

It may seem counterintuitive that, in order to take care of our students, we must first take care of ourselves. There is always so much to be done for our students each day. At least for myself, it is hard to justify taking time, even outside of the school day, to focus on my needs. Yet teachers need to have the emotional and mental space to truly teach and help their students.

The verb in "teacher" is "teach." If we want to do this we must meet our students where they are. Some might say that educators should leave the work of supporting students through trauma to others. But the truth is that teachers are at the front lines of child abuse and endangerment. We are truly the first responders. We see students every day and are in a position of trust. In some cases a teacher is the only adult an abused child trusts; to a child in your classroom you might be the only adult they have a relationship with who is safe and stable. In fact, according to the Department of Justice, "Of all professionals, teachers are the most likely to be told" by a child about abusive situations.

Tell Me Something Terrible

In sharing my students' words, I have been asked if the "I wish my teacher knew" lesson goes too far. Some worry that it might get too personal, might blur the imaginary line between school and home. People wonder, "What if you find out something you don't want to know? What if you find out something terrible?" The truth is, I want to find out something terrible.

My greatest fear as a teacher is that a child will feel forced to hold a painful secret, a secret that if not released could mean they live in fear or harbor a sense of deep shame; that they would be condemned to bear this secret alone. I worry that a child might be going through something I could help with, some trauma that could be addressed if only I knew about it.

The "I wish my teacher knew" lesson is an invitation for these secrets to be released if a student is ready. Children are given permission to open up about whatever they feel is most important. If that means they are brave enough to tell me about a trauma, however terrible, I welcome it.

A fellow educator recommended to many teachers at her school that they try the "I wish my teacher knew" lesson. She told me that of the hundreds of students who completed the activity, about ten children gave answers that were truly cries for help. In one instance, a teenage girl opened up about being sexually abused. When given the opportunity to ask for help, she was brave enough to do so. She is now protected from her abuser and is being given the help she needs to heal.

We want to know kids in all their facets, all their experiences, wonderful and terrible. We teachers want to know the terrible, the heartbreaking, the painful. We do not run away from scary or complicated situations; we run toward them, as a first responder would. We can only support our students in overcoming these difficult situations if we are aware of them.

I am an educator. I am not a social worker or a therapist. I do not have expertise in trauma or abuse. Since that is the case, I know my boundaries. Part of developing my practice as an educator is understanding when and how I can serve students within my own skill set and abilities. If an issue a student brings me is not within ability to support, I seek resources and the expertise of others.

However, as a third-grade teacher, it is always within my capabilities to care for and listen to the voices of the children in my classroom. I choose to be an ally for my students even during times of hardship. By striving to create a trauma-informed classroom environment, I know I can ameliorate the effects of abuse and trauma, which I see as both moral and legal imperatives.

Teachers are truly on the front lines. We act as first responders to identify and report concerns, as well as provide healing to students simply by listening, understanding, and empathizing. As teachers, the relationships we build with students matter. Every day in their very own classrooms our students deserve to have access to an adult who is genuine, consistent, and reliable. We can buffer trauma and prove to students there are adults who can be trusted, so that we can support rigorous learning in our classrooms.

she broke my heart when she declared that my art isn't good enough.

that it was difficult to pay attention in class, not knowing where I was going to sleep at night.

wish my teacher knew I love my family

I wish my teacher knew that I've lived a hard life and I try my hardest and best to remain positive even second of the day

I wish my teacher knew that I've lived a hard life and I try my hardest and best to remain positive every second of the day.

I wish my teacher knew that my mom and dad's argument can effect me and when they do it ruled and my

I wish my teacher knew that moving schools its hard to make friends with people you feel don't like you.

knew my mom might get dangerous with cancer this week and I have been without a home 3 different times this year alone.

I wish my teacher knew that sometimes my feelings and emotions are already crushed when I walk into class and he/she makes it worse by being hostile

I wish my teacher knew that I hated to go back to the other night & it was difficult to pay attention in class

do not pressure kids when they don't even knows going on at home.

I wish my teacher knew I love back

6.
Value-Driven Classrooms
A School Culture
That Develops Character

If you don't work in education, you might not understand what a teacher's job really is. If you think our job is to teach students reading, writing, and math, you're wrong. Teachers teach students, not subjects. We are in the business of growing people by creating situations in which students collaborate, think critically, and solve problems. This requires that our schools and all teachers take an active role in developing the children in our classrooms not only as scholars, but also as human beings with strength of character.

Developing a Moral Code

Psychologists understand morality not in terms of its inherent presence or absence, but rather as something that develops as a child learns and grows. The initial leader in the field of moral development was psychologist and researcher Lawrence Kohlberg. His research, which built on the theories of fellow psychologist Jean Piaget, presented participants with a series of dilemmas and identified three different stages of moral development. While there has been criticism of Kohlberg's work (especially given that it focused on the experiences of Western males), his three stages are a useful tool in understanding how children develop moral reasoning skills.

In Kohlberg's levels of moral development, children begin at a preconventional stage where their moral reasoning is focused on obedience and "avoidance of punishment." Then they shift to look at moral decisions based on the rules of society and how they will be perceived by others. This stage, focused on being "good," is called the conventional stage. We have all had students in our classroom who built their identity around being the "good kid." I once had a girl in my class who was visibly nervous at the thought of "getting in trouble." I talked with her and staged reprimanding her in front of the whole class, just so she could see that making a mistake and being corrected was nothing to fear.

Ultimately, some children will reach a postconventional stage where they examine societal rules to determine what justice means to them and begin to follow "self-chosen ethical principles." It is important to note ethicist and psychologist Carol Gilligan's theory, which adopts the same three levels, but contends morality is care based and that people follow ethics based on their care of others.

Theories of moral development help us teachers understand that morality exists on a continuum. But I also see another key takeaway from analyzing how moral development fits into our classrooms. If we want to develop highly moral students, our goal should not be to create compliant, rule-following "perfect students." Our ideal should not be schools with silent hallways, where students never interrupt. These schools might have obedient students who avoid punishment, but they are not necessarily the most morally developed.

According to this theory, a student with advanced moral development will create their own code of ethics. It might align with the values of the school, but it might also be different. A student with advanced moral development might be someone who questions the authority of a school, especially when the school or its policies are inequitable. And, given the reality of the achievement gap in American schools, it would be hard to make the argument that our nation's schools are equitable. I am not saying that schools should do away with rules or expectations for behavior, but I do think a highly moral school culture might also value productive rebellion based on strong and solid principles.

Impact of Character Education

The term "character education" can be a bit ambiguous, since it is an umbrella term, and because its meaning has changed over time. The US Department of Education has defined it as "an inclusive term encompassing all aspects of how schools, related social institutions and parents can support the positive character development of children and adults." The definition continues: "Character education teaches the habits of thought and deed that help people live and work together as families, friends, neighbors, communities and nations." Character.org, a privately funded nonprofit organization that works with schools, districts, and other organizations to develop character in students, adds that it "addresses many tough issues in

What My Teacher Doesn't Know

Katherine Ocaranza Cortés

All throughout school I was the kind of student teachers loved having in class. Always studious and attentive, I took the utmost care with my schoolwork and participated in clubs and academic contests that extended my learning as far as I could. But, in my senior year of high school, my classmates and I pushed our learning far outside the classroom, so far that we shut down our school—for nine months.

My hometown, Antofagasta, Chile, is a city trapped in a narrow line in between the desolate Atacama Desert and the Pacific Ocean. Our dusty city is filled with hard-working, honest people who are just as stoic as they are generous. It is also filled with a legacy of inequality left by decades of unjust practices in our educational system. In Chile, our schools are capable of providing students with a world-class education, yet we also have extremely high rates of segregation across social classes.

In 2011, the disparity could be ignored no longer. As one reporter put it, there was an overwhelming "perception that Chile's education system is grossly unfair—that it gives rich students access to some of the best schooling in Latin America while dumping poor pupils in shabby, underfunded state schools." So, when I saw university students marching and protesting against this inequity in the streets, I knew I could not stand by and watch other people fight for my right to an education.

My fellow classmates and I began organizing and marching in the streets as well. Though our education was nearly complete, we stood with conviction and demanded that future generations receive a quality education regardless of how rich or how poor their parents might be.

Then, after much debate, a group of classmates and I made the difficult decision to occupy the school. We knew that it meant lessons would be temporarily stopped for students, but in the end we knew that by closing down the school, our cries for change would be heard.

The occupation of our school was not a scene out of a spy movie. Student representatives even discussed our plans in advance with the director of the school. At night, some of my classmates went to the school and wove heavy chains around the doors and clasped them shut with padlocks. During the nights, about thirty students, including me, slept at the school. Each day, hundreds of students arrived on school grounds to attend meetings and help the cause.

At times university students came to teach us about the economic and political pressures that caused the inequality our schools had been experiencing. They taught us about a citizen's role in a democracy and made sure that we all understood the rights and responsibilities of this role. Other times we found creative ways to make our voices heard. Some of my classmates choreographed and performed dances in the central plaza to show our unity. Other times we discussed our dreams for our future and the future of our country.

When the protest started, most of our teachers were critical. Some thought that we were wasting our time, that we had conflated ideas of the impact high school students could make. Others denounced us for halting the education of the younger students. We listened to their criticism and

continues

continued

negotiated an arrangement to continue the occupation of the school while allowing space for younger students to attend their classes.

This compromise earned us respect and support from most of our teachers. Some even marched with us. It was my history teacher who encouraged me the most. He urged me to face issues of inequality head-on. He told me it would take courage to change the educational realities for future generations, a sentiment I will carry with me always.

In the end most of our demands were not met, but this does not mean we failed. We have not yet given up the fight. This whole experience taught me more than any of my school lessons could have. I took this opportunity to apply my academic skills to a worthy cause. I learned how to have meaningful dialogue, how to express my opinions, and how to listen critically to others. Most of all, I learned that a democracy requires action and sacrifice.

I believe in the power of a voice. I believe in change and I believe in people. That is why, in just a few months, I will graduate from university and become a public school teacher. In this way, my fight for a better education for every child has just begun.

education while developing a positive school climate." For me, character education means an effort by the whole school community to positively develop a strength of character that will help students live in our society both today and tomorrow.

Currently, there is no clear consensus on the impact formal character education programs have on student academics or student behavior. The Institute of Education Sciences, the Centers for Disease Control and Prevention, and the Division of Violence Prevention in the National Center for Injury Prevention collaborated to write a 656-page report evaluating the impact of seven social and character development programs (SACD) over the course of three years. The report "did not yield evidence that the seven SACD programs improved student outcomes."

Another publication from Fresno State University reports: "Our research suggests that school goals and activities that are associated with good character education programs are also associated with academic achievement. Thus our results argue for maintaining a rich curriculum with support for all aspects of student development and growth." And a 2013 article in the *Atlantic* stated: "Schools that teach character education report higher academic performance, improved attendance, reduced violence, fewer disciplinary issues, reduction in substance abuse, and less vandalism."

Character education should not be seen as a magical intervention that solves learning and behavior problems. Nor should we justify teaching our students to be positive members of society based on the ability to improve test scores.

As a teacher I strive to model positive character traits and cultivate a supportive culture because it is the right thing to do. My students will grow up to become members of my community, and I want to live in society with people who are caring, hard-working, and resilient. As a state and federal character education advocate Linda McKay says, "I think it's absolutely one of the most critical pieces for education, particularly in

> I wish my teacher knew that sometimes my feelings and emotions are already crushed when I walk into class and he/she makes it worse by being hostile.

high-risk schools; if we don't focus on creating a climate for learning and a classroom culture where students and faculty feel cared for and respected, we won't get to the academics."

Character: An Academic Priority

There is much discussion on how teaching character can predict future success in a student or lead to a student meeting a long-term goal like graduation from high school. This is all true, but we must also look at a more immediate benefit of teaching character education. As a third-grade teacher, it is not possible to teach my students academic content standards if I do not also develop an understanding of character strength, ethics, and values.

Pure and simple, in order to read my students I need to understand the strengths and weaknesses of personal character. After all, the purpose of literature is to reflect humanity back on ourselves, to teach us lessons about our society and ourselves. In Colorado, our schools have adopted the Common Core State

Standards, a move toward more rigorous instruction, which I wholeheartedly champion. We may think these standards are purely academic, but on a closer look, we see that knowledge that comes from character development runs throughout. Of the nine English Language Arts standards for reading literature in third grade, I see direct connections to character education in five.

For example, my third-grade students need to describe the "traits, motivations, or feelings" of characters. In order to achieve that goal, my students first need to have knowledge of, and a vocabulary surrounding, character traits. When I cultivate a shared understanding of courage, determination, and honesty in my classroom, I teach not just the dictionary definition of those particular words. I also help develop the conceptual knowledge and an ability to describe a character in a story, or a person in their lives. Another key standard for my third-grade students is to "determine the central message, lesson, or moral" of a text. I help my students build that skill by intentionally discussing how people, both in real life and in books, overcome hardships and use strategies to solve problems.

More rigorous standards have made developing empathy an academic requirement. My students need to understand that authors, like all people, have beliefs and attitudes. They need to recognize textual evidence that denotes an author's feelings and opinions. When students are able to empathize, that meets another standard: to "distinguish their own point of view from that of the narrator or those of the characters."

I think of a guided reading lesson I recently taught. In order to understand the book, my students needed to read and decode the text, but they also needed to decipher that the main character's actions were driven by jealousy and her motivation

In My Classroom

Luke Morlin, Sixth-Grade Teacher

Our school can only be described as value-driven. Our six core values of respect, responsibility, integrity, courage, curiosity, and doing your best are embedded into everything we do as teachers and as students. We never waste an opportunity to teach character. It is in the books we select, the questions we ask, and even in the vocabulary we highlight. But this year I gained a whole new appreciation for how character education impacts our students.

In the first few weeks of school, teaching my students brought on a new challenge. The students in my homeroom were more diverse than ever before. They were from widely differing economic and cultural backgrounds, had varying levels of academic preparedness, and in addition there was a new level of neurodiversity I had not experienced before.

Our school had just opened a new center-based program to serve students who were impacted by autism, and three of these students were assigned to my homeroom class. As a school, our goal was to fully include these new students into our community and support them in doing rigorous academic work. Achieving this goal was challenging.

These three students had varied experiences with authentic inclusion in elementary school. They were adjusting to learning in general education classrooms like mine, and I was still developing my ability to support them in the unique ways they needed. Due to this, a variety of different social behaviors were displayed in my classroom. One student in particular,

Aiden, coped with his new environment by rolling on the floor, running around the room, and making loud noises at inappropriate times. Honestly, I was worried. I wanted Aiden to get the support he needed but I was also concerned that these behaviors would tear the classroom culture apart.

To respond, I made a renewed effort to focus on teaching character strengths. We explicitly taught lessons on the meaning and necessity for equity and inclusion in our school. We read texts like *Wonder* by R. J. Palacio, a beautiful book with a strong message of tolerance and empathy.

A major part of my approach was identifying students who could become leaders and model empathy and support for students like Aiden. I saw tremendous potential in Jamie. From day one, Jamie had shown an exceptional ability to encourage his peers, once even raising his hand to declare, "Mr. Morin, I think before we start this competition we should all decide to show respect and tell the other team they did a good job, no matter what." Each time Jamie displayed strong character like this, I made a special effort to use his actions as an example for the class.

As the year continued, I saw notable improvements in my homeroom class's behavior. They were adjusting to the rigors of middle school and acting more cohesively, but it seemed that there was still a barrier holding students like Aiden back from participating fully in our community.

One day something amazing happened. Our class was ending the day with our usual routine. Students formed a circle of blue plastic chairs, and one by one students gave each other "shout-outs," where they acknowledged hard

continues

continued

work or kindness they had observed from their classmates. Aiden, however, was on the floor in the back of the classroom, unwilling or unable to participate. Then Jamie made an announcement: "I would like to give Aiden a shout-out."

I seized this opportunity to engage Aiden and called to him, "Aiden there is a shout-out for you." I was a little surprised when Aiden stood up, walked over to the group, and sat in a chair that had been waiting for him. Jamie told the whole class that he was proud of Aiden for doing his best on his math work. Aiden took this information in and then bluntly asked, "Does anyone else have a shout-out for me?" I eyed my students, wondering what this group of eleven- and twelve-year-olds would do. After a short silence, hands shot up. A chorus of compliments followed. From that day on, Aiden's experience began to change at school. He increased the amount of time he was on task and was able to take more control over his disruptive behaviors.

I was proud of my students. By including Aiden and encouraging him, they had taken ownership over the character traits I desperately wanted to instill. But it did not end there. As the year went on, my students' strength of character was working in deep ways that I was not even aware of.

I noticed one particular student beginning to struggle in school. Jiro was a diligent student, but lately he had seemed reserved and withdrawn. I could hardly blame him. As one of the few Muslim students in our school, the year, which had been filled with heated and discriminatory rhetoric from the media and pop culture, had been difficult for him.

I made a point to check in with Jiro often. I wanted him to know that he had someone who would listen to his concerns and act as an ally for him. One day, Jiro opened up to me about the way some students had looked at him that made him feel uncomfortable. I asked Jiro if there were any students in our class who made him feel more secure. I never expected his response.

Jiro told me that of all the students in our class, the one who had helped him the most was Aiden. Apparently one day, unsolicited, Aiden had walked over to Jiro and in the candid way that only Aiden could, said, "I want to tell you I know you're not a terrorist."

"That really meant a lot to me," Jiro explained. "I judged Aiden when I first met him, because he is different. But now I realize he is just a person. And I'm just a person. We are just people. That helps."

I had focused my efforts on getting the other students to make Aiden feel a part of our community, and in the end this empathy and respect resulted in Aiden being uniquely capable of making Jiro feel included. To me, that is the power of teaching our students to have strong values. In the best cases, the students themselves take the values over and demonstrate them in ways a teacher cannot dictate or imagine. You can't measure or quantify this. It will not show up on a test result, but the evidence of strong character will be present in our community. After all, isn't that the purpose of education?

was to be accepted by her peers. Students discussed this and wrote an essay explaining how the author explored the themes of jealousy and friendship. They could not have done this if they were not able to empathize and analyze the integrity of the characters in the story.

Character education and reading comprehension go hand in hand. The complex act of reading requires students to engage with characters in a book in the same way they interact with people in real life. At every level, students must be able to notice the character traits present or absent in the text. They must take note of thoughts and actions that imply a character's emotions in order to make inferences about the character's underlying motivations. These skills are developed when we intentionally develop a child's emotional intelligence alongside their academic abilities. Quite frankly, character education is an academic priority not just for success in the future, but for success every day in my classroom.

Integrated Character

We teachers cannot spend a few minutes a day talking to our students about respect or integrity and think it is going to make a meaningful impact on them. Character education should not be merely a scheduled event; rather, character needs to be woven into every part of our school day.

Good character needs to be part of our school culture and modeled in the way we treat our students and colleagues. This was a lesson learned from the Partnerships in Character Education State Pilot Projects. It was found that "collectively, the states reported that implementation must include the entire school community and be integrated throughout the entire school curriculum and culture."

Possibly the most vocal leader in integrating character education into public schools is David Levin, cofounder of KIPP Charter Schools. David's unlikely collaboration with psychology professor Martin Seligman, professor Angela Duckworth, known for her work studying grit, and private school headmaster Dominic Randolph was profiled in a 2011 *New York Times Magazine* article. It described how the team worked to develop a comprehensive character education program that focused on a "set of strengths that were, according to the research, especially likely to predict life satisfaction and high achievement."

Levin emphasizes a strategy in his schools where teachers explicitly discuss character during lessons. For example, English classes discuss the character strengths and weaknesses of the protagonists in the novels that the class is reading. This helps students recognize their own strengths and weaknesses.

This is a great example of how character education is not just another thing that teachers need to find a way to fit into our already busy day; it is something that should be woven purposefully throughout our day, a sentiment echoed by many.

Timothy Rusnak, a former professor and principal of Ben Franklin High, one of the highest-ranked schools in Louisiana, has stated that "students' attention should be focused on the ethical dimensions of stories, the moral aspects of history, and applying the moral of a story to the student's own life." Bob Chase, the former president of the National Education Association (NEA), said, "We must make an explicit commitment to formal character education. We must integrate character education into the fabric of the curriculum and into extracurricular activities. We must train teachers in character education—both pre-service and in-service. And we must consciously set about creating a moral climate within our schools."

Making the decision to integrate character education consciously is important. The act of learning itself requires a strong character. Curiosity, perseverance, and resiliency are all requirements to acquiring knowledge. Take the time to be deliberate about character in each lesson, whether it is calling out specific character traits from a story or simply closing a lesson with a reflection on how well the school community's values were demonstrated.

Teacher Tools

1. Creating Common Values

In order to teach our students character, each school community will have to define what character means and what qualities the students in their school should strive to embody. This is the first step.

Determining the values you want your students to embody might be more difficult than it seems. There are many dimensions to character. It all depends on which lens you want to look through. You could see character in terms of moral character versus performance character. Character.org has broken down aspects of character in this way. Fairness and generosity are both examples of the ethical values that make up moral character, while performance character focuses more on the individual and encompasses traits like effort and diligence.

Another way to look at character is through relationships. The Institute of Education Sciences categorizes three types of values according to which form of relationship they fit into. First are intrapersonal values, "those characterizing the individual's behavior and attitudes in a wide range of situations and activities" such as honesty, perseverance, and integrity. There are also interpersonal values, which are "characterizing the individual's behavior and attitudes toward others" like caring, respect and empathy. Finally there are civic virtues, which are "characterizing the individual's behavior and attitudes toward the community and society" and include patriotism and justice.

Even more important than selecting character traits to emphasize in a school community is the selection process itself. An analysis of the efficacy of the Character Education State Pilot Projects found that "perhaps the most important lesson to emerge from the Character Education Pilot Project reports was that successful character education requires the participation of the entire community." This sentiment was echoed by education advocate Linda McKay: "What I saw emerging in the research grants [was] . . . that in order for character education to be effective, it really has to be a schoolwide process . . . based on faculty, students, and parents."

I have realized that any character program that mandates a preselected list of values is missing a vital component. The values of a community reflect the entire community and should be determined by all stakeholders. Yes, this includes teachers and school leaders but also students and families. When beginning or expanding a character education program in your classroom, it is wise to ask for input from the students and the broader community, something I'm working toward at my school. Find out what their ideal classroom community would look like, how your community wants to be treated when they are in school, what character traits students want to see in their classmates, and what vision everyone has for their future.

Allowing the entire community to play an active role in determining the values of their school serves two purposes. First, it will create more buy-in from students because everyone is more eager to participate in something they've had a hand in creating. Second, and even more importantly, our students know more about what it is like to be a kid or adolescent in today's world than we teachers do. Our students are experts in the challenges they face, and they can be great sources in pinpointing exactly what character traits are needed to overcome those obstacles.

Students and families have contributions and insights that should be valued when determining the core values of a school community. Schools should keep in mind that these values belong to everyone. As the community grows and changes, the values of a school might need to evolve along with it. I don't mean that a school will all of a sudden stop valuing respect, but perhaps there might be a renewed need to emphasize innovation or creativity. I can also see school culture shifting focus between values that pertain to individuals, such as personal effort, to values with a focus on the community, like collaboration. In this way a school's values might be thought of like a mural, which can be carefully added to or amended over time, instead of as words etched in stone.

2. Common Language

Once the values of a school community have been clarified, a common language can be formed. Building this common language among teachers, students, and community members is the foundation of developing character, but it is often a neglected step.

Most research on shared language comes from the business world and the healthcare industry, where ineffective communication can cost profits or even lives. Interestingly, this research suggests the efficacy of shared language depends entirely on empathy. As stated in the *Australasian Medical Journal,* "Looking [at communication] from the end point of the user helps us to develop empathy, which is a critical factor in building relationships and being able to communicate effectively with others." Yet another reason to incorporate character education in our schools.

Our schools can learn important lessons by examining the way we talk about our values. As teachers we help our students understand the concepts behind our values, like what it means to be responsible. But this clarifying work is also necessary for the adults too. We all come with our own perceptions of values, which are heavily influenced by our backgrounds and the realities of our lives.

The specific words a school uses matter. Think of the nuanced differences between "honesty" and "truth." At my school, our community places a high value on kindness. You will hear that word repeated all over our school. I say, "Can you show kindness and help us clean up?" And during the morning announcements, our principal praises students who have been kind to others at recess. I frequently hear our students compliment each other for being a kind friend. When our students hear the word "kind" from so many sources and for so many occasions, it is powerful.

In our school, a shared language around the value of kindness helps us celebrate exceptional character in our students. Students are able to see kindness in themselves and their peers, but they can also recognize its absence. When students make bad decisions, this shared language helps us have discussions with students that go far beyond "getting in trouble." We can help students understand that a hurtful action is wrong not just because it breaks a rule, but also because being unkind goes against their personal character.

It is also helpful to discuss what your school values would look like in the different settings of your school. Our school does just that. We explicitly teach our students what our values look like in the hallway, on the playground, even in the bathroom. We hang posters that make it clear what our expectations are for their behavior. You can recruit your students to help make these. It's as simple as passing out a few pieces of paper and having groups of students write "Three ways to show gratitude in the lunch line" or "How students can be responsible during study hall."

Schools are made up of so many individuals, but a shared language helps build community. It acts as a bridge that ties the community together and gives us a common identity.

3. Character Rubrics

Teachers are familiar with rubrics to help students evaluate their academic content, but rubrics can also be powerful tools to help them develop strong character. In academia, rubrics have typically been used for the purpose of scoring. The creator of the rubric, usually the teacher, determines the criteria and the dimensions of the product to be assessed. Then each criterion is described for different levels of performance. Usually there are points connected to each level of performance. But there are some important distinctions between a scoring rubric and a supportive character rubric.

There are several character rubrics being used in schools that are great resources. Many of these rubrics evaluate character for students based on the frequency a specific trait is demonstrated. Like one from the Character Counts Six Pillar Program that evaluates if a student "respects authority" always, almost always, usually, sometimes, or seldom. There is an implication that the difference between someone with strong character and someone with weak character is how often that individual exhibits a particular trait or behavior. This is a dangerous fallacy, as even a bank robber could "almost always," for example, "honor people's property." In addition, this form of rubric is not descriptive enough for students. It provides no information on what "respects authority" looks like.

For me, the purpose of a character rubric is to give students a clear picture of what a value looks like in real life. It should give students a judgment-free continuum for a particular character trait or value. This allows them to see that traits like honesty and responsibility can grow with effort over time—and that character can change and grow too. It counteracts the detrimental idea that character traits are fixed.

Another key distinction is that these rubrics are for our students, which means these measures should use language students understand and that is meaningful to them. These rubrics could even be created by students. As teachers we can certainly facilitate the creation of these rubrics to ensure they are accurate and supportive, but the most powerful rubrics will be student directed.

One last note: if the purpose of a character rubric is for students to be able to reflect on their own character and set goals, then quantifying or awarding points to a value might be counterproductive. There is a strong urge in education to make everything data driven, but we need to ask ourselves if scoring a student's character strength is yielding the results we want. Personally, I want my students to self-reflect and think, "I need to work on listening to others so I can understand their point of view" not "I need more points on empathy." The difference between these two thoughts is certainly a result of the way a teacher frames the conversation, but the second we attach numbers to character traits, we are creating a system driven by sums and averages, and that does not always meet our goal of developing strong character.

Teaching our students good character means teaching them the skills they need right now as students, and also to be strong members of the society we will release them into. As adults, our students will need both academic skills and strong character to succeed, but what good is an education that produces students with perfect grades but little integrity? What impact can our students make on the world if they can analyze data and state facts, but do not possess the curiosity and perseverance to ask difficult questions and struggle to seek answers? What type of change would be made, on a global scale, if our schools gave equal focus to developing critical thinking skills and developing a deep sense of empathy?

Educators need to remember this basic truth: our students will grow to become our neighbors, our peers, and hopefully even my superiors. The impact our students have on us might, and should, be greater than the impact we have on our students. It is also true that our students, once independent in the world, will carry with them the values they learned both in their homes and in their schools. With this in mind, I choose to intentionally teach character in my classroom. I can't afford not to.

I truly believe I am educating the children who will become my bosses, my leaders, and my inspiration one day. That belief impacts the priorities of my teaching. I am not only preparing my students to take tests, but I am preparing my students to lead myself and my city. The goal of my teaching is both to develop problem solving skills and the will to solve difficult problems. I expect greatness from my students and therefore also expect pride, tolerance, and resiliency.

Many of my students have already learned aspects of a strong character from their families and communities. It is my goal to build upon what my students have already learned. My classroom acts as an incubator that grows and develops even further the values each student begins the school year with. Over the course of the year I see my students become even more compassionate and more dedicated than when we first met. It's a beautiful thing.

Yes, I need to teach my students academic skills, and I take that responsibility very seriously, but an equal priority for me is to teach them the values that will help form them into the people my community needs and deserves. To me, this is the purpose of schooling.

...she broke my heart when she declared that my art isn't good enough.

...that my teacher knew that it was difficult to say... in class, not knowing where I was going to sleep at night

wish my teacher knew I love my family.

I wish my teacher knew that I've lived a hard life and I try my hardest and best to remain positive every second of the day

I wish my teacher knew not everyone learns the same way! and I wish they knew other people take longer to learn other things!!!

I wish my... it my mom... a argument... effect me... hen they... lled and... knew... to a child...

I wish my teacher knew my mom might get diagnosed with cancer this week and I been without a home 3 different times this year alone.

wish my teacher knew that moving schools its ...rd to make friends ...th people you feel don't ...e you.

I wish my teacher knew that I hated to go back to the school ...y night & it was difficult to ...attention in class

...wish my teacher knew that ...metimes my feelings and ...otions are already crushed when ...walk into class and he/she ...akes it worse by being hostil...

...o not pressure kids when they ...n't know whats going on at ...me.

I wish my teacher knew I love back...

7.

You Got This!

Building a Classroom Culture
of Self-Efficacy

My Classroom Community

I had the pleasure of being the third-grade teacher to an immensely kind and extremely shy girl named Adah. There was no way around it: Adah entered our third-grade classroom with significant academic needs. At home she spoke Spanish with a severe lisp, which her family could understand, but at school the anxiety of not being understood kept her silent most of the time. She almost never raised her hand to answer a question and hardly interacted with the other children in meaningful ways. Adah did not say a single word to me for the first three weeks of school.

But I soon realized these barriers did not stop Adah from working hard. She was rarely absent from school and never missed a single homework assignment during the entire school year. When I worked with her I deliberately and consistently praised her efforts. Each time, I made sure to find an incremental improvement, no matter how small, to show her. I used these

> I whish my teacher knew
>
> I really wantted to be in advance Langye Arts.

successes as evidence to prove to her that she had the ability to learn and grow, no matter how big the challenges seemed to be.

One day, all the students in my class were looking at graphs of their reading achievements over the course of the year. Students were sharing with each other how much their reading had improved and explaining what their new goals would be. I showed the class a student's graph on our projection screen. "Look at how steep this line is!" I said. "This student's reading has shot way up!" The other students looked at it, astounded. One boy shouted, "Whoa! That's crazy!" Others said, "I can't believe it!" With her permission, I finally revealed whose graph it was. "This is a graph of Adah's reading." The class erupted in applause.

Adah beamed silently.

I made it a point in my class to celebrate Adah's growth and her ability to improve instead of focusing on her skill level, which remained significantly below grade-level standards. Through their own hard work and effort, my students prove to themselves that no matter where they start they have the ability to grow and improve. That's how I build and foster a culture of self-efficacy, where every student believes it's within their ability to reach their academic and life goals.

By the end of the school year, the shy little girl who wouldn't speak to me had tripled the rate of her previous academic progress. But even more importantly, Adah demonstrated a huge leap in bravery and confidence when she walked across the stage in front of an audience of thousands to receive the Denver mayor's Mile High Scholar Award.

My teaching philosophy is characterized by the belief that where a student starts does not dictate where they will end up. I don't say this just because it is a nice fluffy thought or because it is what a teacher should say. I could not get up and go to work each morning if I did not see tangible evidence every day that all children can learn, improve, and grow. That word "grow" is at the epicenter of every little thing in my classroom. While I, their teacher, believe in each student's ability to learn, I recognize the need for them to cultivate that belief in themselves.

Just like a plant, there are many requirements that need to be met before a seed can be coaxed to set out roots and a shoot. The belief that one can grow, and that change is possible, is essential to the learning process. Before a student can learn, a sense of self-efficacy must be nurtured within themselves. The American Psychological Association says, "Self-efficacy refers to an individual's belief in his or her capacity to execute behaviors necessary to produce specific performance attainments."

In order to find success in the classrooms, students need to believe they can be successful. Developing a sense of self-efficacy in our students cannot be skipped over or thought of as just another skill that would be nice to teach in the classroom,

if only we had enough time in the day. It is an absolute requirement of learning.

Mindsets in the Classroom

I have been immensely encouraged by research from Stanford professor Carol Dweck. Dweck's research has defined
two distinct mindsets that contribute to the way people, and
especially students, interact with the world: the fixed mindset
and the growth mindset. In the fixed mindset, students believe
their abilities and intelligence are stagnant: they have it or they
don't. In the growth mindset, however, students realize all people have the ability to improve not only their abilities, but also
their intelligence.

So many organizations and industries have latched onto the
growth mindset movement. Education is no exception. Schools
and teachers have embraced it so enthusiastically because we
see students replicate the research every day. We see our students learn, grow, adapt, and become smarter throughout a
given academic year, down to each week and month, even in a
given day.

The best teachers know intelligence and critical thinking
skills are built through effort and rigorous work over long periods of time. More importantly, it is imperative teachers help
students see that as well.

One way to help students develop the growth mindset is to
change the language of a student's self-talk, the voice of their
mindset. Dweck recommends four steps:

1. **Learn to hear how your mindset is expressed in your
thoughts.** Do your thoughts encourage taking on a challenge

or are they overly critical and demoralizing? In our classroom, I use the phrase "Catch that thought, what is it saying to you?" to help students articulate self-talk.

2. **Acknowledging that you always have a choice.** It is so empowering for students to realize they are actually in control of their self-talk and can choose how they think about their abilities as well as how they approach a challenge.

3. **Actively use the growth mindset to talk to yourself.** Instead of students thinking of their failures as proof they are not skilled or competent, coach students to see failures as an opportunity to learn. Helping students understand the way to talk to themselves is key. At our school we even have a bulletin board with fixed mindset thoughts such as "I'm not good at reading" paired with growth mindset thoughts such as "What am I not understanding? How can I work on this?"

4. **Take action.** Once students hear which mindset occupies the voice in their head, can recognize it is a choice, and learn to talk to themselves from the stance of a growth mindset, they are able to use the research in real life. Students will pursue academic challenges as opportunities to learn instead of avoiding them as potential opportunities for failure.

Teaching the students in your room to develop a growth mindset is not nearly as intimidating as it might sound. I go over the idea of a growth mindset with my students and the steps to developing positive self-talk, and then I use the time-honored technique of teachable moments.

When my students say, "I can't do this" I am not annoyed. I revel in the opportunity to challenge their self-doubt. In class one day, I showed students an example of a six-paragraph essay they would be writing. Six paragraphs to third graders, many of whom would be writing in their second language, might as

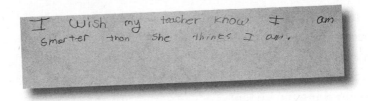

I wish my teacher know I am smarter than she thinks I am.

well have been a Greek epic. I saw the self-doubt in their faces as their eyes widened and lower lips dropped.

"What are you thinking?" I asked.

"That's so long." a student commented.

"I won't be able to do it," admitted another. I encouraged my students. I actually had the whole class say, "This is going to be hard. I will at some point get frustrated and I might even get bored, but I will write this essay."

This was a brief interaction with my class. However, repeatedly modeling this ideology, coupled with strong instructional methods, helps students develop a growth mindset. My students see they are able to accomplish difficult tasks. After several days of strategic instruction, every one of my students did write their first essay, and they also developed a sense of self-efficacy. "Notice," I said, "that sometimes when you think you can't do something, you really can."

Are We Modeling Optimism or Pessimism?

The way our students interpret and respond to setbacks and challenges is a major component of self-efficacy. Part of living from a growth mindset is the belief improvement is possible with sustained effort. The other part is explicitly teaching students they have the ability to accomplish goals. To do this, we must nurture the endless power of optimism.

Optimism is not just seeing the glass as half full. In a psychological context, optimism and pessimism are seen as reflections of how people explain life's events to themselves. Optimistic people believe difficulties in life can be overcome, while a pessimistic person interprets challenges as permanent.

A person's tendency to be more pessimistic or optimistic has been shown to greatly affect their life. In his 1995 book, *The Optimistic Child,* Martin Seligman summarizes his research and points out the dangers of pessimism saying, "Pessimism is an entrenched habit of mind that has sweeping and disastrous consequences: depressed mood, resignation, underachievement, and even unexpectedly poor physical health. It hardens with each setback and becomes self-fulfilling."

Whether a person is optimistic or pessimistic can often be picked up on by others, especially children. Theories in cognitive psychology suggest "that one way people learn is via social learning. That is, people emulate and duplicate behaviors that they observe in their environment." As teachers we know our students are not only studying the curriculum, but they are studying us as well. That means we need to be models of optimism.

Our daily thoughts and actions need to demonstrate to students that thinking positively about the world, seeing our setbacks as temporary and changeable, helps us achieve our goals and become more productive and more effective people.

Building Gritty Students

Complementing Dweck's and Seligman's transformative research on optimism is Angela Duckworth from the University of Pennsylvania. Duckworth claims there is a quality beyond

In My Classroom

Amy Lyon, Fifth-Grade Teacher

I was eager to further explore character education in my classroom. When I started learning more about grit and the tremendous role it plays in our lives, I knew not only was this skill essential, but it was also something I could teach in the classroom. For my students in rural New Hampshire, I developed a yearlong curriculum, one lesson every month, to understand and develop grit.

My students began the study of grit with a discussion of the concepts of optimism and pessimism. For my students, I explain that optimism is about facing adversity realistically and then taking action to deal with it. We dive into the idea that the more optimistic someone is, the more likely that person is to be able to do "deep practice" to get better at something of his or her choosing, which leads to perseverance. That, to me, is the foundation of grit.

The first thing I notice in my classroom is the change in language. Kids start talking about a task as a "challenge" instead of simply "hard." I actually hear our students explaining to their friends what their long-term goals are and the steps

intelligence or socioeconomic status that contributes to students' success. Her research states that some students possess a quality that allows them to overcome adversity and stick with difficult pursuits for prolonged periods of time.

She calls this quality "grit" and has defined grit as the "disposition to pursue very long-term goals with passion and

they will need to take be successful. It is evident that students are more aware of how to manage schoolwork when it
gets hard. I see students working harder to solve more rigorous problems because they see struggle as proof that they
are challenging themselves.

As a capstone project, our students create a Perseverance
Walk. I ask students to think about an adult they would like to
interview about how that person accomplished a long-term
goal. Together we generate potential interview questions
around three major topics: the goal set by the interviewee,
the obstacles overcome in the process, and finally what the
interviewee's life is like after obtaining his or her goal.

With this information, students can create any number of
products to show their learning, such as a poster, slide presentation, essay, or even produce their own video. However
they choose to present their Perseverance Walk, the sense
of pride students have as they show off a goal that someone dear to them has accomplished is palpable. This lesson
serves as tangible proof for students that lots of ordinary
people have goals and with that come hardships. The real
difference is in how you choose to manage those hardships.
Will you give in or will you show grit and persevere?

perseverance." Her research has found that students with more
grit attain higher levels of education, earn higher GPAs, and are
more likely to graduate from high school. With outcomes like
that, actively teaching grit should be a part of every classroom.

Lyon's Perseverance Walk is one specific lesson teachers can
implement in their classrooms. It shows that integrating grit

> 3 things I wish my teacher knew about me.
>
> 1. 7 kids in my family, me being the 2nd to yongest.
>
> 2. I play basketball
>
> 3. I think I'm really good at writing

does not have to be separate from our academic curriculum, but rather that teaching self-efficacy skills, like grit, can be academically rigorous and complement our curriculum, as well as become incredibly meaningful to students. As teachers we can deliberately look for teachable moments to identify grit to our students and value it as an academic skill.

Teacher Tools

1. High Five Goodbye

The end of the school day is typically pretty hectic around Room 207. There is homework to be distributed, tables to wipe down, and inevitably something that slipped my mind until one minute before school gets out. I am working toward making the end of the day a calm and tranquil time, but I have found one thing that helps students, so I leave on the right foot even if it is a little chaotic.

On the way out the school door, I stand at the bottom of the stairs and give each of my students a high five. As our hands meet, each student repeats back a positive affirmation, like "I am a world changer!" or "I can be kind to others." No matter how the day went, no matter how challenging it was, my students and I end with saying something positive. This helps model optimism for them.

Even though this takes just a few seconds, I have found that this little goodbye, simply a short phrase or sentence, helps to validate the work the students have done and leaves everyone, including myself, feeling just a little better. On a practical level, it has the added benefit of pacing out eager-to-leave students so they do not trample each other in the hallway.

Sometimes I come up with the High Five Goodbye phrase. I like to tie it to what we have learned that day, like "I can fight for justice like Dolores!" after learning about civil rights activist Dolores Huerta, or "I'm as strong as the Rocky Mountains" when we study geography. Other times I will call back to something our students struggled with that day, like "I can control my body" or "Kind words matter." Most often, I have students come up with the phrase themselves. They have said things like "I am a respectful kid" or "I've got power in me."

Whatever the phrase of the day, it is important to emphasize that effort, hard work, and character matter in our classrooms. The High Five Goodbye is just one simple way of doing that.

2. Coach and Response

Teachers have been using the call-and-response technique in their classroom since . . . well, since forever. Usually I have seen this used as a way to get attention. When I was a student, my teachers used the tried-and-true "One, two, three . . . eyes on me," with students responding "One, two . . . eyes on you" to quickly get the attention of the class so they could give directions.

I get my students' attention in much the same way, and it works. In addition I also use what I call a Coach and Response. Its purpose is not to grab attention, but to encourage students, while they are actually doing their work, to use their very best effort and push themselves even when the work is challenging. Students don't stop work and look at me; they yell out their response, which lights a little fire in their bellies, so it's easier to keep going. They are encouraged to persevere and develop grit.

For example, when students are writing a paragraph independently, everyone starts off on task and are all working, but then the little murmurs begin. The writing is getting a little harder and students are tempted to play with their erasers or talk about the football game at recess. That's when I use a Coach and Response. I will shout out, "Can't stop!" They will yell back—and I require it to be loud—"Won't stop!" I follow up with "All day!" and they respond, "Every day!"

This simple two-second exchange acts as a reset button. Students get a small reprieve from being silent and it reminds the class they are expected to work hard. I see their little nostrils flare, their eyebrows lower in concentration, their faces move just a little closer to the paper or computer they are using.

The Coach and Response can literally be anything, but it should matter to the class. This year, we stole Denver Broncos' quarterback Peyton Manning's play call. I said, "Hurry, hurry!" Then students yelled, "Omaha!" What that actually means is a total mystery, but to our football-obsessed students, it is motivating. I have heard teachers use lyrics from songs and funny quotes from students. Three years ago, one of my students came

Here are some calls I use in my classroom:

Teacher	Students
Can't stop . . .	Won't Stop
All day . . .	Every day!
Are you ready?	I was born ready!
Never give up!	Never surrender!
Refuse . . .	To be distracted.
These hands . . .	Will change the world! *clap *clap
Dale . . .*	Con ganas!*

*Loosely translated from Spanish to "Give . . ." "Your best effort!"

up with his own and said, "What are we? . . . A community!" My current students still use that Coach and Response in our class!

Angela Watson, National Board–certified teacher and host of the *Truth for Teachers* podcast says, "When I lived in DC, I taught many children from Nigeria and Ghana, where call-and-response techniques are deeply rooted in the culture and extend beyond the classroom walls. "Ago . . . Amée!" (pronounced AH-go, AHM-ay) is a great example to use in the classroom. Hold the notes a little bit (Ahh-gooooooo . . . Am-éeeeeeee!)." This is a wonderful way to build community and value the cultures our students bring to school. Get creative and come up with your own Coach and Response!

3. College Fridays

While there are certainly other pathways to academic success, attending college can be seen as the epitome of a learning career. Whether a student would become the first in their family to study at university, or a college education seems like a forgone conclusion, attending and graduating from college is a shining example of a long-term goal that requires grit.

One October, buried deep in a email, I saw that Denver Public Schools was celebrating College and Career Readiness Month, and I decided our students needed to celebrate it in our classroom as well. I began by asking a simple question to my students: "What is college?" Kara's hand shot up to save the day. Kara was a wonderfully ambitious student reading a year above grade level in her second language. She excitedly answered, "I know! College is the same thing as sixth grade!"

Some of my students know about colleges and universities. Some have parents or older siblings who have graduated from college. And some have families who talk about college as an expectation. But for many of my students, college is an unknown concept. If our students are going to attend college, they need to learn about it at an early age. In this spirit, my class began the tradition of College Fridays.

Starting College Fridays was surprisingly easy. I enlisted my colleagues to wear college T-shirts on Fridays. One year, teachers even made their own college pennants out of construction paper and hung them in the hallway with pictures of their college days lovingly glued to the edges. I have sent students running around the halls with clipboards, interviewing every teacher and adult they see, asking, "Where did you go to college?" and "What college would you want to go to?"

The most important part of a College Friday in my classroom might also be the simplest. As we end our week of learning on Friday afternoons, we take the last few minutes of school and look up a college video online. We watch admission commercials for colleges my students have heard of, maybe colleges family members have gone to. We even look up college sports and study-abroad opportunities. One Friday, Ariela presented me with a crumpled-up piece of paper that had been in her pocket all day. She said, "I asked a lady at church to write down the name of this college so we could look it up." Then Matthew said, "My brother is in the JROTC," the high school–level armed services training program. "Can we look that up too?" Soon College Friday grew into High School Thursday and Middle School Wednesday. We even started looking up careers and jobs students were interested in. Soon, our students' curiosity had created an uncomplicated career education program.

All of this turned into a meaningful and much-anticipated time for our students. They started talking about colleges like they were their favorite colors or sports teams, saying things like "I call dibs on the University of Chicago" and "Janet and I are going to be Ducks at the University of Oregon together."

There is power in ending each day and each week with a deliberate conversation about students' futures. It helps connect their learning to their future goals. Our class knows we are not learning fractions because they're on the test. We are learning fractions because they help us understand the world, and we need to understand the world if we are going to do great things. More importantly, a genuine discussion of future possibilities tells students they have the ability to accomplish their goals.

4. You Can Get Away with It

I tell students they can get away with anything in my class. Yes! I tell them that, but I do so to emphasize that learning is a choice. I start by pointing out that they already made the choice to come to school. I say, "You chose to come to school to get your education. You chose to come to school today because you know that learning gives you power. Our class needs you here. Thank you for making this choice."

Even in elementary school, but especially as they get older, students really can choose to show up for school or not. We can punish students or incentivize them to learn, but at the end of the day it comes down to each student's personal choice to pursue learning. Acknowledging that choice gives students power. It clearly places accountability in a student's hands and goes beyond just physically being present in the classroom. Making the choice to learn takes grit, and we should call that out for students.

A major part of my reading instruction is sustained reading. This means students are reading books for enjoyment and practicing literacy skills we have discussed, for forty-five minutes to an hour, each and every day. In my classroom, each and every child practices what our class calls "power reading." Some students lie on desks, sit in comfy beanbags, or sit back-to-back with a friend. One particular student liked to read hanging upside down draped over a chair. Regardless of how they sit, I expect each and every one of my students to be reading. The challenging thing for me as a teacher is that reading is a 100 percent a choice for my students. I can enforce that they hold a book and sit quietly, but I can't jump inside their brains and make them sound out words. I address this choice in deliberate ways.

As a class we make charts that compare and contrast "power reading" and "fake reading." Students act these out and see if their partners can tell the difference. I tell my students the story of Joe, a former student, who was a very skilled reader. He came into third grade able to read the more challenging texts better than any other student in class, but as the year went on he struggled to make the choice to read. Instead of pushing himself, he chose the easiest books he could find. Often he was just holding a book, looking at it but not making the choice to read. Joe did well in third grade. He passed every assessment, but he could have done so much better if he had consistently made the decision to do the hard work of reading.

In reflecting on this, I think about moves I could have made to engage and encourage Joe to make the choice to read, and being honest with students about the choices they have is one change I have made in my instruction. Now I tell my students, "You can be just like Joe. You can go through third grade and get away with not actually reading. I might not catch you right away, but know that you are making a choice." As a class, we talk about their personal reasons to make the decision to learn. My students this year even wrote an essay explaining why they wanted to become power readers.

I see my students make an active choice to learn, not just demonstrate compliant student behavior. What's more, I see students encouraging their peers to make that same choice. Choosing to learn takes grit. It takes perseverance and resiliency, and we need to tell children the truth about this. In an age of school and teacher accountability, we are missing something if we don't teach our students that they are the ones who need to take ownership of their own learning.

5. Labels Are for Cans, Not People

One night, I was at a party chock-full of teachers. With a room like that, we could have only been discussing one thing:

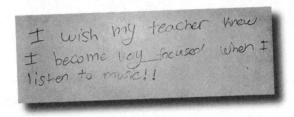

I wish my teacher knew
I become very focused when I
listen to music!!

school. One man made a comment about the success he had
found in his classroom with an "autistic student."

Another teacher at the party said, "You know you should
really say 'student with autism.'"

"Why? Just to be politically correct?"

She replied, "No, it just makes sure that we are talking about
the student first, not their diagnosis or disability. It's just a few
extra syllables, you'll get used to it."

As teachers we label students all the time. We use acronyms
and proficiency bands as shorthand, saying students are "un-
satisfactory" or "advanced." We have all heard terms like "good
kid" and "problem student." In our data-driven instructional
worlds, our students are placed into buckets, each with a cor-
responding label.

Yes, teachers do need to be able to categorize in order to
group students with similar needs so we can deliver highly tar-
geted instruction. We also need to leverage the different abilities
in our classrooms. We need to be able to describe the barriers
affecting our students, but I argue that we can do this in ways
that do not put fixed and self-determining labels on them.

I propose we get honest with ourselves as educators. Chart
out all the labels we put on students—all of them. Root out all
the little ways we describe students in conversation, in documents, in test scores. List them all. It would be wonderful to do
these activities with colleagues, but you could just as easily do

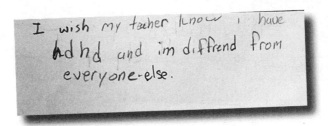

I wish my teacher know i have
Adhd and im diffrend from
everyone-else.

them as an individual teacher. Then decide. Is this a label we want to keep, eliminate, or change?

I do not have definitive changes to make for all these labels, but I am interested in starting the conversation about it. That being said, I feel there are strong arguments for changing and eliminating some of these labels. It might serve students well to completely eliminate highly charged labels.

Our assistant principal at Doull Elementary, Rob Suglia, has a background in teaching students who qualify for special education services. "When I taught middle school students, my job was to support students who had documented learning disabilities and also to support general education teachers. Yes, I taught students who had individual education plans and, technically, my position was 'special education teacher,' but to the students I was Mr. Suglia, another math teacher." When he told me this it was like a lightbulb turning on.

Why can't we refer to a special education teacher as a "fifth-grade teacher?" There is power in this, says Suglia: "We placed a strong emphasis on coteaching. A team of teachers planned together and truly collaborated. In this way, both the general education teacher and the special education teacher were equals. That equality and collaboration is what we want to model for all students."

With this in mind, I believe the education community should reimagine the term "gifted and talented." To me, it does not seem

Label	Keep	Eliminate	Change to:
High students			
Low students			
Privileged			
Underprivileged			
Unsatisfactory ("Unsat")			
Gifted and Talented			
Limited English Proficiency			
Smart			

appropriate. To begin with, who is giving out the gifts? And why have so few of my brilliant students received this golden designation? In some situations, the "gift" these students receive seems highly correlated to which zip code they live in, which language is first spoken to them, or how much income is in their home.

That's not to say there aren't students out there with tremendous skills that need to be supported and pushed. I know some of our students have different needs, and sometimes they need to be challenged in a different way than their peers. While we have a real need for this extension to traditional classroom work and professional expertise, labeling some students as "gifted and talented" (in essence defining their skills as passive and fixed) implies that other students are not. This does not fit with what we know about the ability to improve one's intelligence and skills, or the inclusive communities we are trying to create.

The labels placed upon students are not benign; they affect our students and our teaching. We owe it to students to carefully consider the language we use. Labels are for cans, not people. By being deliberate and intentional about all labels issuing from our classrooms, we can help empower our students. What's more, we can allow students to believe in their own ability to accomplish their goals.

5. *Choose Your Level*

I have discovered that there is nothing third-grade students want more than to be fourth-grade students. Similarly, third-grade students want desperately to distinguish themselves from their younger second-grade peers. There is something magical about that one day that changes us from one grade to the next. We all remember that single day when we became a mature, sophisticated high school sophomore and could look down with pity on the clueless freshmen.

I discovered this when I was having my students use a rubric to evaluate their writing. In the rubric, I gave my students real examples of what a particular essay would look like at four different levels. But I didn't label each category with a number (1, 2, 3, and 4). Instead, I wrote "1st grade, 2nd grade, 3rd grade, 4th grade." This worked well because "3" or "3rd grade" was the level of proficiency I wanted them to achieve.

During the lesson I said, "A second-grade essay would have a basic topic sentence, while a third-grade essay would have a clear topic sentence that gives the reader context, and a fourth-grade essay would also have a clear topic sentence that gives the reader context but also lays out the organization of the essay." I knew I was onto something when I was interrupted by a student who asked, "But what would a fifth-grade essay have?"

What My Teacher Doesn't Know
Aswad Allen's Story

Throughout my life, I have been honored to support so many dedicated students. As assistant dean of Diversity and Inclusion at the University of Colorado at Denver's School of Education and Human Development, it has been a special privilege to help develop teacher candidates. While I can't think of a better way to spend my days than helping our students and teacher candidates on their path to becoming educators and mental health professionals, when I look back on my own schooldays, I cannot think of a career that was more unexpected for me.

As a young child, a traumatic event led to me experiencing a severe speech impediment. My anxiety caused me to stammer over nearly every word. Every part of school became challenging. I could not communicate with my teachers, tell them what I understood, nor could I ask for help when I needed it. Educators responded to this by placing me in special education instruction.

Once being labeled a special education student, I became overwhelmed by a feeling of despair. Even as a young child, I could see that the students I was grouped with had challenges different in nature than mine. Not being able to communicate and believing my speech problem would keep me from ever being heard terrified me. I worried the day when I would finally be heard would never come. That fear quickly transformed into something much more debilitating: embarrassment and shame. Feelings resulting from having been labeled only served to keep me quiet longer.

The term "special education" was accurate. I did need a form of education that was different and more supportive than did some of my peers. But it was the label itself that did the most damage. At the time, it seemed like it would determine my fate. I thought that my single challenge of communication was enough to overshadow all of my strengths. I could also sense the low expectations my teachers had for me. It would have been easy to allow the label of "SpEd" student to define me, but thankfully my parents had a different vision for my life.

In middle school, I had the opportunity to start over with different teachers and a different school. By that time, my stammer was less present, but still I was behind academically. These issues impacted me when I started high school. At the new school I was made to repeat the ninth grade. Psychologically, this led to yet another label: "retained." Being held back made me feel isolated, and yet it gave me a tremendous amount of personal responsibility. I began to realize it was completely up to me, and me alone, to overcome these challenges and create a new reality for my life.

With personal persistence and the help of very caring teachers, I was able to overcome the labels placed on me. Graduating from high school and being offered scholarships to attend college affirmed I belonged. I've been in school ever since.

Now I am able to leverage my unique perspective to help others find an appreciation for students who, like me, learn differently. I encourage our teacher candidates to rethink the expectations and assumptions they make about their students. We can empower students when we allow them to define their own identity and set their own goals. The most powerful thing a teacher can give their students is a "voice" in deciding who they are.

Since then, I have used this method to let students choose their own goals. For important skills my students absolutely need to master before the end of the school year, I simplify my rubrics to only three categories: second grade, third grade, and college.

Here is a real example from my classroom:

Skill: Composing a sentence that clearly describes the central message, lesson, or moral

Second Grade	Third Grade	College
In this story, the lesson is when ____ you should ____.	In the text, the lesson the author wants to teach the reader is when faced with ____, you should ____.	It is clear the central message the author attempts to illuminate through the text is when one ____, one might ____.

Allowing students to choose their own level creates motivation for improvement. It teaches them how to set and achieve goals specific to their abilities, in the moment. No longer is their writing good, bad, or almost. It is a matter of choosing which level a student is choosing to work at. Students are remarkably good at self-selecting the level that is best for them.

Using this system, I rarely have to encourage students to challenge themselves, because the format itself requires them to take charge of the level of work they produce. By offering students choice and a clear path to the next level, they develop self-efficacy while being provided the motivation to constantly get better and move up levels.

Good teachers believe in their students' abilities; great teachers teach students to believe in their own abilities. We only have our pupils for a finite amount of time, which means we plant the seeds, yet rarely see the harvest. As educators we cannot merely teach content or standards. We must teach our students how to learn, and that means we need to teach them that they can learn, that they already possess the ability to progress and improve. This trait is essential if we want our students to become lifelong learners.

By teaching a growth mindset and developing soft skills like optimism and grit, we encourage students to develop the confidence of a learner and be accountable for their own education. When we take the time to deliberately and explicitly teach our students to have a strong sense of self-efficacy, we cultivate a community of learners that can't be stopped.

she broke my heart when she declared that my art isn't good enough.

wish my teacher knew that if was difficult to pay attent in class, not knowing where I was going to sleep at night

WISH MU eacher new I ve m famile

I wish my teacher knew that I've lived a hard life and I try my hardest and best to remain positive every second of the day

3. I wish my teacher knew when to keep teaching or stopping to tell us a story.

wish my f... st my mom a a argument a effect me a hen they do alled and my

I wish my teacher knew my mom might get diagnose with cancer this week and I been without a home 3 dif times this year alone.

wish my teacher knew at moving schools its rd to make friends, th people you feel don't e you.

I wish my teacher knew that I hated to go back to the school y night & it was difficult to pay attention in class

wish my teacher knew that metimes my feelings and notions are already crushed when walk into class and he/she akes it worse by being hostil

I wish m teacher knew I love back

o not pressure kids when they ork bent whats going on at ome.

8.

"I Can't Wait to Learn More"
Classrooms Where Student Engagement Thrives

My Classroom Community

As quickly as I could, I slammed the doors of my classroom shut. Once again, my students were being way too loud. I wanted to avoid the embarrassment of the wonderful fourth-grade teacher crossing the hall and patiently shutting my door so her class could get their work done.

I had given my students an assignment to take measurements by using nonstandard units, like how many shoes long a table is. Frantic groups of students were measuring and recording the lengths of as many classroom objects as they could in ten minutes. Then the plan was to have the groups compare measurements. Through discussion, students would arrive at the conclusion that mathematicians cannot invent their own units of measure.

But the process was loud.

Students were shouting at their group mates, "The chair is four hands tall!" or "Let's see how many pencils high the ceiling is!" Kids were standing on tables trying to measure doorways by backpack lengths and running around the room to see who could measure the bookshelf first. It was chaotic.

Then my principal walked in. I froze. She was quickly followed into the classroom by a woman I did not recognize. "We heard the noise from outside and decided to come in," my principal explained as several students raced passed her.

"Oh no, are we being too loud?" I asked apologetically.

"What are they doing?" The woman asked, gesturing to a group of students lining up markers along the windowsill.

I explained the idea behind the lesson and asked again, "Are we being too loud? Should I make them stop?"

"Hmm," she said, "They certainly seem engaged." My principal and the woman observed for a few more nervous minutes while the students fervently ran around measuring every object. Then they slipped out.

Perhaps if I had not been a first-year teacher at the time, I would have recognized exactly what the situation was. I might have known that strangers who enter your classroom wearing impractical shoes, and with a suspicious absence of magic marker or glue stick stains on their clothing, are usually people who work in the school district office. I might have realized the stranger was actually my principal's boss completing a mandatory classroom observation of the novice teachers.

That afternoon, I anxiously asked my principal how the classroom visit went. She told me she was glad to see the students so enthusiastic about their schoolwork and that she was impressed that every single student was on task, collaborating, and discussing their work with each other. But then she told me it was probably not a good idea to allow students to stand on the tables—a fair point.

I wish my teacher knew....
Sitting so long makes MY legs hurt.

This experience was one of many that taught me how essential student engagement is in any classroom, and made me grateful that I worked in a school where this was valued. Ideally, a classroom is not a place where students are always compliant and silent. Sometimes highly engaged classrooms can get a little loud and hectic. An engaged classroom is a place where students can't wait to do the hard work of learning, and to me that's worth the temporary noise and chaos.

Why Engagement Is Essential

When I was in school, I was not engaged. I didn't know I was supposed to be engaged. I thought my role as a student was to do my work, get good grades, and do my best to avoid getting in trouble. Like many others, I took a pragmatic approach to my education. The best-case scenario was acquiring the best possible grade by expending the least amount of effort. It wasn't until I had decided on a personal goal of becoming an effective teacher that I truly engaged in my own learning. I saw so many of my classmates have the same disconnected experience in school, but I certainly do not want this for my students.

According to a report from the Institute for Research and Reform in Education, "There is general agreement that engagement in learning is as important for success in school as it is elusive in the vast majority of traditional, bureaucratic school structures." The same report found that "by high school as many as 40 percent to 60 percent of students become chronically disengaged from school—urban, suburban, and rural—not counting those who already dropped out."

As teachers, we can feel how engaged students are in our classrooms. There is an excitement and an energy. On the best days, students can't keep themselves from asking questions and are reluctant to go to recess because they need to read just one more page. We also see the opposite when we have to bribe students into doing their best, cajole a class into paying attention, or beg them to just sit still for a few more minutes. Like me, maybe you have found yourself wondering, "I spent so much time on this lesson, why aren't my students excited about it?"

This contrast is perfectly described in an article in *Educational Leadership*: "Most teachers have seen these signs of engagement during a project, presentation, or lively class discussion. They have caught glimpses of the inspired inner world of a child, and hoped to sustain this wonder, enthusiasm, and perseverance every day. At the same time, they may have felt stymied by traditions of reward and punishment. Our challenge is to transcend these very real difficulties and provide a practical model for understanding what our students want and need."

The term "student engagement" has taken its place among the most popular buzzwords in education. The most prominent researcher focusing on student engagement is former public school administrator, professor, and founder of the Schlechty Center for Leadership in School Reform, Phil Schlechty. In his book *Engaging Students,* he defines student engagement as having four characteristics. First, engaged students are attentive and on task. Second, students who are engaged are committed and do their work voluntarily. Third, students persist in their work even when it is challenging. Finally, engaged students find meaning in accomplishing their work. These characteristics beg the question, how do we engage students? How do we get them to a place where they are displaying visible joy in our classrooms and authentically incorporating their learning into their lives?

Relationships Matter

The relationships we build with our students matter. They allow us to know who our students are, what they need, and how we can best support them. But it's a two-way street. What we put into our relationships with our students comes back to us in the form of student engagement.

Researchers from Portland State University found that "over time, warmth, structure, and autonomy support from teachers and peers not only operate as social resources but also help students to construct their own personal motivational resources by promoting positive self-perceptions of relatedness, competence, and autonomy. Students can draw on these resources when they encounter difficulties, coping constructively, re-engaging with challenging academic tasks, and in general developing everyday motivational resilience."

This is a big responsibility for teachers but it is also an opportunity. The type of relationship we build with our students becomes the foundation for their performance in our classrooms. Each time I show care and interest in my students' lives, I am

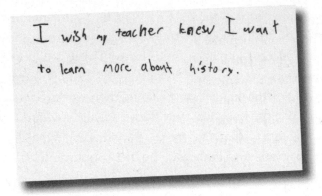

I wish my teacher knew I want to learn more about history.

building an interpersonal link that creates the support system they need to feel connected to their schoolwork. For me, it is comforting to know that the effort I put into knowing my students as people and learners really does contribute to their ability to engage in difficult educational tasks.

Teacher Tools

1. Acts of Service

Service learning can be seen as a teaching philosophy. The National Youth Leadership Council describes service learning as "an approach to teaching and learning in which students use academic knowledge and skills to address genuine community needs." That can sound intimidating, but you don't need to change your approach to teaching to incorporate service.

In our school, students have collected food for the homeless. They have organized penny drives for cancer patients and held shoe drives for people in need. One year, students even hosted a schoolwide yard sale that raised money for an animal shelter. These actions make an impact. Framing activities like this, no matter how small, as Acts of Service for our students gives value to the academic skills they learn in school.

I saw this firsthand in my classroom. One year, I read the book *Beatrice's Goat* to my students. I never expected the way the story affected my class. The book tells the true story of Beatrice, a girl living in Uganda, who receives a goat from the nonprofit Heifer International that allows her to support her family and attend school. As soon as I finished the last page, my students asked if we could send a goat too.

Sending the goat was a powerful learning experience. They worked together to come up with ideas to raise money. We ended up making and selling bookmarks and holding a bake sale. They came up with a pricing scheme and used multiplication to figure out how much we would have to sell at what price. Certain students were in charge of adding up all the coins and dollars and reporting the amount to the class. They had to figure out how much money had been raised and how much more we needed to meet our goal. In the end, my students didn't collect enough money to send just one goat. They actually raised more than enough, so they had to decide what to do with the extra money and persuade their classmates of their plan.

It was such an exciting project and one that I cannot take much credit for. The experience was student driven. I was really just along for the ride, facilitating their work but not directing it. My students set their own goal and decided how to achieve it. This allowed them to collaborate and work creatively to solve a genuine problem.

Each student had a unique talent to contribute. Some drew intricate designs on the bookmarks and some baked cookies with their families; still others kept track of the finances. Completely unsolicited, two students made crafts at home and sold them at our bake sale. I was not even responsible for providing the motivation. My class connected with Beatrice's story and wanted children like her to go to school. It was my students' empathy that provided the true motivation.

The whole project fit so well with Schletchy's four characteristics of student engagement. They worked attentively and with commitment. Together, my students showed persistence and were able to contribute something meaningful, not just to their own education but to the world. To me this embodies not only student engagement, but also student empowerment.

There are so many ways to incorporate Acts of Service into your instruction. Our schools provide a natural opportunity for students to provide an Act of Service simply by sharing their knowledge. There are always younger students whom your students can teach. Instead of hanging your students' work outside their classroom, display it for younger students. My students have made posters explaining how the human body functions and then hung them outside the kindergarten classrooms. This little change turns a routine assignment into something much greater. In the same vein, I have turned reading a short play into an opportunity for my students to entertain their classmates. Students have also planted seeds during a science unit with the end goal of supporting our community garden.

The ways to make Acts of Service part of your classroom are infinite. Turning schoolwork into meaningful contributions to the community helps students understand that their learning has a purpose beyond completing tasks and acquiring points. When the work students do in our classrooms helps real people and solves real problems, we have truly engaged them.

In My Classroom

Lauren Fine, Elementary Teacher and Dean

Education is not just my profession; it is my passion. In the last decade each experience in urban education has taught me how to be a better educator, but it was the time I spent volunteering at a school in Accra, Ghana, that changed the way I viewed my role as a teacher.

Although the lives of the students I worked with in Ghana were extremely challenging, their desire to learn was unquenchable. Every day I saw their passion for learning, and yet I was also confronted with the harsh reality that their access to education was limited due to an inability to pay school fees.

Inspired by these students a fellow educator, London Moore, and I decided we wanted to respond to this inequity. We solicited donations from our family and friends and were able to send ten students to school in our first year.

Over the next three years, our efforts grew into a small nonprofit called the Ghana Educational Collaborative. We not only provide school fees to students with high academic standing, but we also provide leadership training, and mentorship. Now, three of our graduates attend university. I credit much of our success to one of our students, William.

I remember the first time I met William. At the time, he was a driven sixteen-year-old eighth grader who, due to financial barriers, was forced to halt his education several times. William exemplified the purpose of our program, embodying the

continues

continued

grit, determination, and intelligence our organization hoped to support in our scholars.

Almost immediately William became much more than a scholarship recipient; he became a true partner in our work. William helped us understand the nuances of working in Ghana and assisted in the day-to-day operations of the program. Once we hit a roadblock in transferring the payments for school fees. So, we sent funds directly to William. He crisscrossed the city and distributed the money to each school in time to keep every student in school.

In our second year, we knew our students needed stronger mentorship, but being so far away it seemed there was little I could do. William took the initiative to mentor the younger students and began leading "family meetings" every month. At these meetings students gathered to discuss their school progress, develop leadership skills, and support each other through challenging times. When I think about authentic engagement and leadership, I think of how William has been a part of our work every step of the way.

His impact reached far beyond the work in Ghana; it extended right into my classroom here in the United States. Seeing the leadership and ingenuity this young man brought to our organization made me rethink parts of my role as a teacher. I became aware of how often in impacted communities, programming happens "to" our students, and not "with" our students. I realized I needed to give students, like William, a place at the decision-making table.

As an elementary school teacher, I know my students can positively impact the community as much as I, or other adults, can. In order for students to be fully engaged and invested in their learning, I realized that I could not merely be their instructor; I needed to be a true partner in their education.

This led to a program I started in my classroom called Little People, Big Changes. Each year, my students create a service project where they can apply their academic skills and make a real difference. One year, my students researched the impact that limited access to books has on reading abilities. They raised money to donate books to the preschool students at the Head Start program across the street. Another year, my students collected shoes and sent them to students in need.

It is a powerful thing when students see themselves as little people who can create big changes in this world. My students know the skills they are developing as readers and writers have an authentic purpose: to impact and improve the world in which they live. This is what can happen when we teachers ask our students not just to engage in our classrooms, but also to be engaged citizens of the world.

I choose to actively elevate the voices of students, both in my classroom and in our scholarship program. When you allow students to be the drivers of change, you allow them to recognize the power they have. This is the lesson that William taught me.

What My Teacher Doesn't Know
William Yakah

I don't know where to start. I guess everything begins in Dabala.

Dabala is a typical village in the Volta region of Ghana. There was no electricity and just one elementary school. In order to be admitted to the school, you have to be old enough. In Dabala, being old enough is not measured by your age. Instead, each child must prove that he or she is physically big enough to start school. At the start of each school year the principal lines up the children of the village for an arm test. You must reach your right arm over the top of your head and touch your left ear. If your fingertip can touch your ear, you may begin your education.

I couldn't wait to go to school like my older brothers. I was small for a six-year-old, but I eagerly lined up with the other children and reached my right arm as far as I could. The principal pointed to the centimeters between my fingertips and my ear and sent me home for another year to sit at home, help in the fields, and do the impatient work of growing.

During that year, each day I forced my brothers to yank on my right arm in an anxious attempt to gain the centimeters that kept me from my education. When the next arm test came, my arm was still a few stubborn centimeters from where it needed to be. But hope was not lost. I had practiced inching up my shoulders and tilting my chin ever so slightly forward so that my arm would appear to be longer. That is how I outwitted the principal and earned the opportunity to start my education.

Sitting in the dusty school room was like an intense thirst finally being quenched. I reveled in learning that the tangled lines on the page were really letters and numbers. And, if you learned to untangle them, you would be rewarded with knowledge.

When I was nine years old, in search of work our family moved from Dabala to Accra, the capital city. At times, my parents could not provide the school fees. My brothers and I took turns each year. One of us would attend school while the others worked to support the family. I would not be deterred. This was my chance. I would do anything to make the most of my education.

One day in school, a teacher showed me a photograph that caused me to realize a dream I didn't know I had. In the picture there was a man with a white jacket and blue pants. It said "doctor." From that moment on, I knew I was meant to be a doctor. That vision for my future motivated me to commit myself entirely to my education.

I began waking up at 3:00 a.m. each morning. I left the one-room shack my family lived in, walked through the tightly knitted homes to quietly study under the dim light of a lamp-post. As the years went on and high school grew closer and closer, the reality set in. I had no way to pay the fees and my dream of becoming a doctor seemed farther out of reach than ever.

Then the Ghana Educational Collaborative came into my life. They offered to pay my fees, buy my textbooks, provide a stipend as well as mentorship from their board members. I was determined to make use of this opportunity, to achieve

continues

academically, and pursue my seemingly impossible dreams. I wanted to develop as a leader and become a person who could help others.

I had not merely earned a scholarship. I had become a part of the GEC community. I began mentoring the other students in the scholarship program, checking in on them and tutoring them with their schoolwork. Honestly, the relationship I formed with my fellow students helped me just as much as it helped them. When I told them how much I believed in them, how much I expected from them, and how their hard work would result in their success, these are the words I needed to hear as well.

I want teachers to know that the inner drive we students need to fully engage in our education comes from a clear understanding of the journey we are on. Students like me need to have a vision for our future. In every lesson they teach, educators need to help us conceptualize the connection between what is being taught and its relevance to our world and our dreams of the future. We students need help to hold on to the dreams that can pull us through our challenges. That connection is what drives us to overcome our challenges and work harder to keep our dreams alive. Each skill we learn along the way is really a step on our journey to pursuing our dreams. That journey can take us to the most incredible places. I am proof.

Education has taken me, a small boy from the hinterland in Ghana, across the ocean to study at Michigan State University, the beginning of the realization of my dream towards becoming a doctor. As I work to achieve my dream, I also work to ensure that there are more students to follow.

2. Family Learning Projects

The idea for Family Learning Projects came from fellow teacher Tiffany Martinez. She and I were leading a group of second-grade students in an intense study of insects as a part of our school district's summer English Language Acquisition Academy. Ms. Martinez invited her students to create a bug diorama at home.

This had not even crossed my mind. If I'm being honest, I hadn't thought of inviting my students to complete this type of project, largely because of my own biases. My perspective of creating a diorama came from the way I had done it as a child. My parents had driven me across town to a craft store and spent $20 on plastic figurines, paint, and fake grass. I thought this extra expense for a school project might not be accessible to all of my students. Due to this flawed assumption—that some students and their families would not have the resources to complete an assignment—I simply didn't offer the opportunity.

I am grateful that I was proven wrong when, day by day, Ms. Martinez's students showed up at school beaming with pride as they carried a Styrofoam spider or a poster with the body parts of a ladybug carefully labeled. Her students had the same challenges as mine. But because Ms. Martinez gave her students the opportunity to create something meaningful, they took their learning further than mine did. After this realization I invited my students to do the same project and was amazed by the results. Though my students had varying levels of resources and family support, each and every one brought in a bug project that showed their unique personalities and interests.

Two brothers actually collected live ants to show the class. One boy told me he didn't have anything at home to do the project with, so I sent him home with a few sheets of construction paper. He came back the next day holding a colorful menagerie of carefully folded origami butterflies and cockroaches.

Ever since this experience, I have incorporated Family Learning Projects into my classroom. I have learned a few key aspects that have helped make them successful. One is to make these projects optional and ungraded. Even though they are not required, most students still complete the projects. Each time a student brings in a project, it is like free advertising motivating more and more students to go home and give it a try. I also leave it up to the student to decide if they would like to publicly present their project to the class. They almost all choose to stand at the front of the class and share, but I don't see the point in forcing students to engage in public speaking if it causes them extreme discomfort. I also do not see a need to grade the projects. The purpose is for students to take the learning we have done in class in whatever direction they choose. Making Family Learning Projects graded would mean that I would have to create grading criteria, and in this case it might stifle creativity.

This leads me to the next aspect of my Family Learning Projects. They are completely and utterly open to interpretation. The assignment sheets I send home say something like "We are learning about the planets. Create an interesting solar system project. There are no rules. Have fun!" I have also sent home a single sheet of paper with one simple printed sentence: "Turn this into a paper airplane." Students have complete freedom to create these projects and I have been amazed by the results.

One of our Family Learning Projects was to make a map of Colorado. Some students drew pictures and others made posters. A student who loved computers made a digital map with his father. Another even made a completely accurate map by decorating a sheet cake with her mother. For our solar system

I wish my teacher knew, I love animals and I whould do anything for my animals. I whould love to work at the mspca so I could help animals get adopted

project, one family created a glow-in-the-dark solar system complete with an electrical circuit. Another student who had limited supplies at home brought in a solar system made completely out of the materials she had: a box she found in our classroom recycling bin and her most precious resource, her Halloween candy.

The best part for me is when families help bring in the projects. The adults are just as excited as the students to show off the projects they worked on. Seeing the faces of my students' mothers, fathers, or aunties glowing with pride at their child's work shows me the impact of these projects.

Family Learning Projects offer something my third-grade students have likely never had in their education career: complete freedom to investigate a topic they are interested in and demonstrate their knowledge in whatever way they see fit. I have found that the only thing students and families need in order to do this is a simple invitation. As teachers, sometimes all we need to do to engage our students is provide the opportunity.

As I have grown as an educator, my strategies for engaging students have evolved. I know I have the ability to manufacture student interest in my classroom simply by being amusing. I can stop a book right at a cliffhanger and leave my students pleading for more. I can make silly faces or jokes so they hang on my every word. Just by putting a piece of technology in front of my students, I can keep them on task and absorbed in their work. Most teachers know how to grab their students' attention, but remember that true engagement is not entertainment.

When it comes to student engagement, the truth is we are already set up for success. All students want to learn. All students want to grow. We do not need to trick or bribe them into learning. We want our students to passionately pursue knowledge not just because we said so, but also because learning is the deepest of human desires. We only need to provide the space, time, and opportunity for them to explore their interests and passions. We need to give our students a chance to develop skills so they can make a real impact on their community.

Conclusion

My experience in posting my students' "I wish my teacher knew" notes taught me a lot about the power our classrooms hold. First it taught me the power of sharing. For years, the students in my classroom told me exactly what I needed to know. But I kept the lesson to myself. Once I shared the lesson, I became aware of just how far one simple question could travel. Right now there are so many lessons, so many ideas and insights inside our classrooms just waiting to be shared with the larger educational community.

I have also learned the power of the shared experience. So much of learning is universal. Teachers the world over have shared with me their own experiences with "I wish my teacher knew" notes. In countless languages, students have bravely shared their truth with the caring adults who teach them each day. All teachers want to connect with students. All students want to be heard. In every corner of the globe, this is the intersection where relationships are formed.

When we stop seeing students as problems to be solved, we can begin to see the children we teach as valuable partners in problem solving. That's when the relationships we build in the classroom transform into partnerships. Students can tell us what is important, what is necessary, and what we need to know about their lives to effectively educate and engage them.

As teachers, we need to remember that the relationships we form hold so much influence with our students. Haim G. Ginott, teacher and school psychologist, realized just that, as he stated in his classic book from 1975, *Teacher and Child*:

> I have come to the frightening conclusion that I am the decisive element. It is my personal approach that creates the climate. It is my daily mood that makes the weather. I possess tremendous power to make life miserable or joyous. I can be a tool of torture or an instrument of inspiration. I can humiliate or humor, hurt or heal. In all situations, it is my response that decides whether a crisis is escalated or de-escalated, and a person is humanized or de-humanized. If we treat people as they are, we make them worse. If we treat people as they ought to be, we help them become what they are capable of becoming.

The Stockdale Paradox

Admiral James Stockdale, a true American hero, was captured and tortured during the Vietnam War. Despite all odds, he survived the horrific ordeal, reunited with his family, and was awarded the Medal of Honor. While Stockdale's plight is much different in nature, his triumph can still teach educators a powerful lesson about the mindset required to prevail even in the most difficult of situations.

Stockdale recounted his experience to business consultant Jim Collins, who then described it in his book *Good to Great*. The admiral credited his ultimate success to his unwavering belief that, in the end, he would make it though. "I never lost faith in the end of the story. I never doubted not only that I would get out, but also that I would prevail in the end and turn the experience into the defining event in my life, which, in retrospect, I would not trade."

While Stockdale makes it clear that his commitment to a positive resolution was essential, he is quick to point out that he never lost sight of the severity of his situation, saying, "You must never confuse faith that you will prevail in the end—which you cannot afford to lose—with the discipline to confront to the most brutal facts of your reality."

Collins calls this duality the "Stockdale Paradox." He describes it in his book as the ability to "retain faith that you will prevail in the end, regardless of the difficulties *and* at the same time confront the most brutal facts of your current reality, whatever they might be."

Our nation's schools face a brutal reality. More than half of the children in our nation's schools are living in poverty. Our schools are more segregated by race and socioeconomic status than they were before the Civil Rights Movement. Schools that serve a disproportionate share of students living in poverty must stretch already thin resources to serve a disproportionate share of students with disabilities and students of color. This means that our students who need the most often get the least. More students in our schools than ever before are tasked with learning academic skills while simultaneously learning to understand English. Despite having the largest economy in the history of the world, America has not been able to build a public education system that, as a whole, can compete with the rest of the developed world.

It is essential to have a realistic assessment of the failures of our public education system. As educators we cannot shy away from this. We cannot sugarcoat the realities our students and our schools face. We must be critically aware of the challenges our students face as well as the policies that have created and contributed to those challenges. In doing this, we can become powerful members of the educational community and strong advocates for our students.

As the Stockdale Paradox warns, it is ineffective to exclusively focus time and energy on the fact that our society and our schools suffer from so much injustice. There is more to education than just constraints. As teachers we have a real ability to make a positive impact in our classrooms. The relationships we create not only support students during trying times, but also can motivate them to achieve great things and make an impact on the world. Our students have so many strengths we can build on. Even in consideration of the poverty and trauma so many of them face, we can form classroom environments that develop strong character and empathy. The ideas our students explore in our classrooms today will become the basis for their contributions to our society tomorrow.

Both these things are true: our American education system has historically and is currently failing many students *and* we can prevail in the end to create schools worthy of the incredible students who fill our classrooms. We must never lose faith in the goal that every classroom, regardless of the challenges we face, can become a powerful community of learners. When we accomplish this goal, it will be the defining achievement of our generation.

Each time we give a student a voice we work toward a better reality. Each time we comfort a student in the midst of pain, each time we encourage a student to struggle through difficult work, each time we give students an opportunity to discover their passions, we nurture our faith that we can meet the true goals of education. Our schools can produce resilient, creative, and passionate learners who will improve our world.

I have a realistic assessment of the challenges and barriers our schools and our students face. Yet I continue to have the unwavering belief that we as teachers, as a community, as a country can give every student the excellent education they deserve. I do not suffer from believing the fallacy that I cannot make a difference. I make mistakes, I get it wrong sometimes, but I am committed to reflecting and growing each day. And I expect the same from the children whom I am entrusted to teach. My students have a very real ability to impact the world. That, in the end, is what I make sure my students know.

I Wish My Teacher Knew
A Teacher's Guide

The Lesson

There are many ways that the "I wish my teacher knew" lesson can be adapted to suit a particular classroom's needs or educator's teaching style. Depending on the dynamics of the students involved, the lesson itself can take between fifteen and forty-five minutes. But the impact stretches far beyond that.

1. Set the Purpose

Start by explaining to your students how important it is for teachers and students to form relationships. Depending on your students' age this could be as simple as "I care about you. I want to know more about you so I can be a better teacher." If students are older, you may want to share some of the research presented in this book. Explain that many issues affect learning, and that you as a teacher would like to know what life is like for the students in your classes.

2. Be an Example

It is helpful to share your own school experience with students. Each teacher can determine the extent to which this is appropriate. You can share your personal struggles and triumphs or simply keep it brief, but at a minimum you should share what you wish your teachers had known when you were in school. This makes the experience reciprocal. You share with them and they share with you. You may even consider completing the sentence "I wish my students knew . . ." for the class.

3. Make the Options Clear

One of the beautiful nuances in the sentence "I wish my teacher knew . . ." is that it allows students to take their answers in any direction. They are in control. Many of my students answer the sentence with what could be seen as surface-level answers, saying things like "I wish my teacher knew how to play soccer" or "I wish my teacher knew I love dinosaurs." I will be the first to say that these answers are just as valid and valuable as any other response. All of my students' responses help me learn important information about their passions and interests.

Other times, my students' responses reveal something deeper, like an emotional struggle or a trying family situation. It is perfectly fine to explicitly tell students they are in control of how detailed their responses are. Tell students it's okay to write something funny or serious, happy or sad, or to not write anything at all.

I even tell my students that I welcome their feedback on my teaching. Students can tell me something they appreciate about our class, but I encourage them to share something they feel needs to change. I also invite them to write as many notes as they would like. Some students write me three or four notes. This allows students to share as much or as little as they want with their teacher.

4. Sharing Out

The very first time I had my students complete the "I wish my teacher knew" exercise, I simply passed out Post-it notes, wrote the words on the board, and collected what they handed in. What I have learned over the years is that the exercise is much more powerful when it is completed not as a quick assignment, but rather as a community activity.

One of the greatest surprises for me was how willing and enthusiastic my students were to share what they had written, even when the content was deeply personal. One year, my students asked to share their responses with the rest of the class. I gathered students in a circle on our colorful rug. Hands shot up. Some students even whined that I was not calling on them fast enough. I encourage teachers to allow willing students to share their responses if it makes sense in their classrooms.

Sharing has been a powerful component to the lessons in my classroom. For one, it has allowed students to get something off of their chest. One girl shared, "I wish my teacher knew I am always so nervous." Another boy said, "I wish my teacher knew I don't think kids like me." Confessing these concerns removes the weight of isolation. Even if a child chooses not to share their thoughts, they benefit from listening to others. I once had a student who was shocked to find out that other students in her class also had parents who had gone through a divorce.

Listening to classmates' sentences gives students the opportunity to practice empathy and also participate in problem solving. When one of my students shared that he feared other students did not like him, several classmates were able to encourage him. They said, "Oh, I like you!" and a chorus of "Me too" filled the room. "Are you sure?" he asked timidly. Students chimed in with all the reasons why they liked him. The whole episode ended with a group hug that toppled over onto the floor.

5. Allowing for Anonymity

Sharing the notes as a class was deeply powerful in building community in my classroom, but it is also important that students have the ability to keep their names separate from their messages, if they choose. To account for this, I give them a few different options.

1. You can read your note out loud to the class.
2. I can read your note out loud to the class and keep your name private.
3. You can leave your note in a box and I will read it privately.

Providing these three options gives students a choice in how their messages are shared with their teacher and class. I also tell them that they can add "Talk to me about this" at the bottom of their notes. For example, if a student discloses "I wish my teacher knew my parents are getting a divorce" and then adds "Talk to me about this," I will know whether that student simply wants to inform me of their situation, or if they'd like my active support.

It should be said that true anonymity is a difficult thing to offer students. Unless a teacher is deliberately using technology, most educators can differentiate between students based on their handwriting alone. Figuring out who forgot to write their name on a worksheet, year after year, has made most teachers expert in handwriting analysis. I think it is fair to tell students this. Older and more sophisticated students will figure it out anyway, and your admission of the limitations of the assignment can help to build trust.

Teachers and students alike might be concerned about how the sensitive content of their response will be handled, like students sharing they are having thoughts of suicide or are being victimized in some way. Teachers should be aware that as mandatory reporters there is a possibility a student might share something that will require action to be taken. In some circumstances it might be appropriate to share this reality with students.

In my classroom, if a student expresses concern about what they write being secret I explain that I can keep their note private, but that I will also do what I need to keep them safe. Avoid statements like "No matter what you say, it stays between you and me" or "What students share in this room will stay in this room." These are not promises any teacher can, or should, keep.

6. Closing with Community

Ideally this activity is completely student driven and therefore it will look different in each classroom. No matter how a lesson takes shape, closing it in a way that builds community in your classroom is essential. Using our judgment as teachers, there are several forms the ending of this lesson can take. Students can share their thoughts, offer encouragement to their classmates, or discuss ideas the classroom community can use to support each other.

Sometimes as teachers we think there is an understanding in our classrooms. As teachers we will listen to anything our students need us to know. However, our students might not share the same understanding. Even blanket statements like "You can always come to me" or "I will always be here for you" do not go far enough. Be explicit with your class. Tell them it is your job to help them learn, and sometimes that means supporting them with issues that happen outside of school, like a divorce in their family or not having food at home. I explain to my students in sensitive and age-appropriate ways that if they are ever in a dangerous situation, I am a person they can talk to. My students are also told that I need to know what they are passionate and curious about. I want to know what their goals and dreams for the future are. Do not let these things go unsaid.

7. Repeat When Needed

I have been asked several times how often a teacher should do this activity. The answer is as many times as will be helpful. If the activity works for your class once, try it again. If there is a significant event or school change that affects your students, try the activity again. You might invite your students to write what they wish their principal knew, or even what they wish their president knew.

To ensure that "I wish my teacher knew" is more than just a class activity, leave the door open for dialogue. I have seen teachers continue the conversation by placing a real mailbox in their classrooms and explaining that students can write her letters at any time. I have added a question to the end of a quiz asking, "Is there anything you wish I knew about this unit?"

The bottom line is that our students have triumphs, curiosities, and concerns they want to share with us—which they sometimes need to share with us. As teachers we have the power to engage our students in this meaningful conversation whenever it is needed. Keep the "I wish my teacher knew" lesson with you as a tool.

Join the #IWishMyTeacherKnew Community

When I shared my students' voices through their "I wish my teacher knew" notes, I found something very powerful: a community who listened. Since posting the first note online, I have heard from so many teachers who have shared the lesson and found the same success in their classrooms that I found in mine. I have a sneaking suspicion that there is a big opportunity here for educators to teach each other.

I urge everyone who reads this book to share what works in their classrooms and communities because, while every child is unique, so much of our educational and school experiences are universal. What works in one classroom may work in many. Let's allow the ideas and voices of our students to inspire even more educators and impact the education of children across America.

Join our community today by visiting IWishMyTeacher Knew.info and by using the #IWishMyTeacherKnew hashtag on social media. Together, we can turn our students' wishes into realities. We can talk, share, and dream. And we can give every child the excellent education they deserve.

Acknowledgments

There are so many people who deserve acknowledgment for helping to make this book a reality. Thank you to Lynn Johnston, my agent, for envisioning this book in the first place. I would also like to thank my editor, Dan Ambrosio, as well as Matty Goldberg, Kevin Hanover, Lissa Warren, Sean Maher, Miriam Riad, Christine Marra, Renee Sedliar, and everyone at Da Capo Press for championing a book that would encourage teachers and support students. I would also like to extend my gratitude to my collaborator, the smart and dedicated Meghan Stevenson, who motivated and guided me as well as helped me form my ideas in this book.

To the many people and organizations who helped me on my path to becoming a teacher, thank you. Thank you to City Year and AmeriCorps, whose work does as much good for its members as it does for our nation. In particular, I would like to recognize a special kindergarten student who became the highlight of my time at City Year and the spark that made me want to teach. Also, thank you to the English Opens Doors program and the generous community in Antofagasta, Chile, who welcomed me. I must also acknowledge the Denver Teacher Residency, which has worked so hard to develop teachers worthy of our brilliant students in Denver. To the Glowmundo organization, which has provided such inspiring character lessons, thank you for your dedication to our students. Thank you to the Fulbright Program for the wonderful learning opportunities I was given to connect with educators in China. I would also like to thank America Achieves, the Colorado Educator Voice project and the #TeachStrong movement for helping me find my voice as a teacher and the confidence to share it.

As a proud Denver Public Schools teacher, I would like to thank all the people who make Doull Elementary such a wonderful place to teach and learn, especially our compassionate principal Jodie Carrigan, who gave me the opportunity to teach in such a strong community. Thank you also to all my fellow teachers at Doull, who dedicate themselves to giving our students an excellent education. I'd like to especially thank Kathy Brougham for being not only a strong colleague, but also my mentor and friend. Thank you also to the families who have supported my classroom and given me the privilege of teaching their children. And thank you to all of my students. Each of you possesses so much power. It is a joy to see you use it to change the world.

I would like to thank all the teachers and students who have lent their voices to this book, some of whom I have known for many years, and some of whom writing this book has provided me the opportunity to learn from. You have given everyone who reads this book so much to consider and so many reasons to continuously improve our schools.

To educators around the world who have humbly asked their students the simple and powerful question, "What do you wish I knew?" Thank you for listening to the voices of your students. And to the students who have bravely answered, thank you for speaking out. I must also acknowledge those from near and far who have heard of this project and offered so much encouragement. Your support has kept me going on difficult days.

I owe a thank-you to the friends and family members who have offered me unwavering support and encouragement, including Benafsha Shroff, J. J. Schuber, Molly Couture, Valerie Wintler, Rachel Bernard, Samone Imani Moore, Rachel Roe, Lauren Fine, Angela Cobian, Jay Galbraith, and Gilbert Blythe. Thank you for listening, asking questions, and providing insight. I would also like to show appreciation for my strong faith community at Platt Park Church for embodying hope and light for me and so many others in need.

Finally, I would like to thank my family. To my grandmother Darlene Schwartz who always makes sure I know I am cared about. To all the Schwartzes and Galbraiths out there who make up the best family anyone could ask for, thank you. I would like to thank my lovely sister Katelyn who has always paved her own path and provided me with footprints to follow. Finally, I have a tremendous amount of gratitude for my parents—my father, known to all the students at our school as Coach Ken, and my mother, Cathy—who have always encouraged me and loved me deeply.

I love you all very, very much.

Notes

Introduction

2 *90 percent of our students lived in poverty* Doull Elementary School Spotlight Summary Scorecard, http://spf.dpsk12.org/documents/current/227%20-%20Stoplight%20Scorecard.pdf.

2 *"No significant learning . . ."* Ruby Payne, "Nine Powerful Practices," *Poverty and Learning,* Educational Leadership, April 2008, 48–52, http://www.ascd.org/publications/educational-leadership/apr08/vol65/num07/Nine-Powerful-Practices.aspx.

Chapter 1. Welcomes and Farewells

18 *61 percent of students* The Early Childhood Longitudinal Study, https://nces.ed.gov/ecls/.

18 *16 percent of fourth-grade students* Russell W. Rumberger, "Student Mobility: Causes, Consequences, and Solutions," University of California, Santa Barbara, June 2015, http://nepc.colorado.edu/publication/student-mobility; http://nepc.colorado.edu/files/pb_rumberger-student-mobility.pdf.

18 *"students who changed schools . . ."* "K-12 Education: Many Challenges Arise in Educating Students Who Change Schools Frequently," GAO report number GAO-11-40, December 20, 2010, http://www.gao.gov/assets/320/312484.html.

19 *"involuntary moves..."* Russell W. Rumberger, "Student Mobility: Causes, Consequences, and Solutions," University of California, Santa Barbara, June 2015, http://nepc.colorado.edu/publication/student-mobility; http://nepc.colorado.edu/files/pb_rumberger-student-mobility.pdf.

20 *first month's rent* "K-12 Education: Many Challenges Arise in Educating Students Who Change Schools Frequently," GAO report number GAO-11-40, December 20, 2010, http://www.gao.gov/assets/320/312484.html.

20 *witness these evictions firsthand* Personal conversation with a teacher in the Denver Public School District who wishes to remain anonymous.

20 *dealing with several of these issues Reading on the Go! Volume 1: Students Who Are Highly Mobile and Reading Instruction,* National Center for Homeless Education at SERVE, prepared for the National Center for Homeless Education by Patricia A. Popp, The College of William and Mary, December 2004, http://center .serve.org/nche/downloads/reading_on_the_go.pdf.

21 *family member being deported* Center for Public Integrity, http://www.publicintegrity.org/2013/03/14/12311/mental-health -study-us-kids-affected-surge-deportations.

22 *homelessness is on the rise* Education for Homeless Children and Youth: Consolidated State Report Data, School Years 2010– 2011, 2011–2012, and 2012–2013, September 2014, http://center .serve.org/nche/downloads/data-comp-1011-1213.pdf.

23 *their living situation* Military Child Education Coalition, https ://secure.aacte.org/apps/rl/res_get.php?fid=1256&ref=rl.

23 *80 percent of military-connected students* US Department of Defense Education Activity Enrollment Report, http://www.dodea .edu/datacenter/enrollment_display.cfm.

23 *a military-family life counselor* Personal conversation with a De- partment of Defense employee who wishes to remain anonymous and has had her name changed here to Sandra Temple.

24 *Individualized Education Plan* AASA "5 Things School Lead- ers Can Do to Promote Academics," http://www.aasa.org/content .aspx?id=9012.

25 *Interstate Compact on Educational Opportunity* Military Child Education Coalition, http://www.militarychild.org/the-interstate -compact-on-educational-opportunity-for-military-children-see.

26 *mobility does have an impact* Russell W. Rumberger, "Student Mobility: Causes, Consequences, and Solutions," University of California, Santa Barbara, June 2015, http://nepc.colorado.edu/ publication/student-mobility; http://nepc.colorado.edu/files/pb_ rumberger-student-mobility.pdf.

26 *A 1996 study* David Kerbow, *Patterns of Urban Student Mobil- ity and Local School Reform.* Published in October 1996 by the Center for Research on the Education of Students Placed at Risk,

Baltimore, MD, and sponsored by the Office of Educational Research and Improvement, Washington, DC, http://files.eric.ed.gov /fulltext/ED402386.pdf.

26 *support from peers and teachers* Diana H. Gruman et al., "Longitudinal Effects of Student Mobility on Three Dimensions of Elementary School Engagement," *Child Development*, Nov–Dec 2008, http://www.ncbi.nlm.nih.gov/pmc/articles/PMC3870003/.

31 *the Welcome Kit a bit further* Personal conversation with Molly Couture.

34 *what happened to my family* Personal conversation with Julian Roldan.

37 *"Kids need closure . . ."* Personal conversation with Susana Moening.

Chapter 2. Students and Poverty

43 *51 percent, of all the children* Motoko Rich, "Percentage of Poor Students in Public Schools Rises," *New York Times*, January 16, 2015, http://www.nytimes.com/2015/01/17/us/school-poverty -study-southern-education-foundation.html.

45 *". . . food-insecure children . . ."* *Too Hungry to Learn: Food Insecurity and School Readiness*, Children's HealthWatch research brief, http://frac.org/pdf/national_school_lunch_report_2015.pdf.

46 *In My Classroom, Valerie Wintler* Personal conversation with Valerie Wintler.

48 *224 billion meals* National School Lunch Program Fact Sheet, US Department of Agriculture, September 2013, http://www.fns .usda.gov/sites/default/files/NSLPFactSheet.pdf.

48 *qualify for free meals* National School Lunch Program: Trends and Factors Affecting Student Participation, Food Research and Action Center, January 2015, https://nces.ed.gov/programs/digest /d12/tables/dt12_046.asp.

49 *an hourly wage of $9.97* Minimum Wage Laws in the States Wage and Hour Division (WHD), US Department of Labor, January 2016, http://www.dol.gov/whd/minwage/america.htm#Colorado.

49 *defined by the United States Department of Agriculture (USDA)* National School Lunch Program, USDA, http://www.fns.usda.gov/ sites/default/files/NSLPFactSheet.pdf.

50 *What My Teacher Doesn't Know, Briti's Story* Personal conversation with Benafsha "Briti" Shroff.

52 *American Society for Nutritional Sciences* Diana F. Jyoti, Edward A. Frongillo, and Sonya J. Jones, "Food Insecurity Affects School Children's Academic Performance, Weight Gain, and Social Skills," *Journal of Nutrition,* December 2005, http://jn.nutrition.org/content/135/12/2831.full.

52 *ranked seventeenth in the world* PISA Results in Focus 2012, Organisation for Economic Co-operation and Development, http://www.oecd.org/pisa/keyfindings/PISA-2012-results-US.pdf.

53 *"In schools where 75 percent . . ."* Cynthia McCabe, "The Economics Behind International Education Rankings" *NEA Today,* http://neatoday.org/2010/12/09/a-look-at-the-economic-numbers-on-international-education-rankings/.

53 *the best and worst schools* Mel Riddile, "PISA: It's Still 'Poverty Not Stupid;'" National Association of Secondary School Principals School of Thought, http://blog.nassp.org/2014/02/12/pisa-its-still-poverty-not-stupid/.

54 *effective community development efforts* John P. Kretzmann and John L. McKnight, *Building Communities from the Inside Out: A Path Toward Finding and Mobilizing a Community's Assets* (ACTA Publications, 2006).

58 *Totes of Hope* Programs for Children, Food Bank of the Rockies, http://www.foodbankrockies.org/programs/programs-for-children/.

59 *Feeding America's Food Pantry Program* Jodi Gibson. "School Pantries: Helping Kids Thrive at School," Feeding America, http://www.feedingamerica.org/hunger-in-america/news-and-updates/hunger-blog/school-pantries-helping.html?referrer=https://www.google.com/.

62 *Backpack Index* Huntington Bank press release, http://huntington-ir.com/ne/news/hban072915.htm.

64 *barriers to eating breakfast* USDA School Meals: Community Eligibility Provision, http://www.fns.usda.gov/school-meals/community-eligibility-provision.

65 *80 percent or more students* No Kid Hungry Center for Best Practices, https://bestpractices.nokidhungry.org/school-breakfast/school-breakfast-policy-0.

66 *impact of these programs* Breakfast in the Classroom, Food Research and Action Center, http://frac.org/wp-content/uploads /2009/09/breakfastforlearning.pdf.

67 *Emily Griffith* Phyllis J. Perry, *Bold Women in Colorado History* (Mountain Press Publishing, 2012).

Chapter 3. All Families Count

71 *2000 and 2010 US Censuses* James Nye, "1 in 3 U.S. Children Live without Their Father as Number of Two-Parent Households Falls by 1.2 Million in Ten Years," *Daily Mail*, December 26, 2012, http://www.dailymail.co.uk/news/article-2253421/1-3-US-children -live-father-according-census-number-parent-households-decreases -1-2-million.html.

72 *families are more "ethnically . . ."* Natalie Angier, "The Changing American Family," *New York Times,* November 25, 2013, http://www.nytimes.com/2013/11/26/health/families.html?page wanted=all&_r=0.

72 *voluntary kin.* Dawn O. Braithwaite et al., "Constructing Family: A Typology of Voluntary Kin, *Journal of Social and Personal Relationships,* May 2010, http://spr.sagepub.com/content/27/3/388 .short.

72 *divorce rate is on the decline* Natalie Angier, "The Changing American Family," *New York Times,* November 25, 2013, http:// www.nytimes.com/2013/11/26/health/families.html?page wanted=all&_r=0. Brittany Wong, "The Truth About the Divorce Rate Is Surprisingly Optimistic," *Huffington Post,* December 2, 2014, http://www.huffingtonpost.com/2014/12/02/divorce-rate -declining_n_6256956.html.

73 *6,441 children were adopted* Intercountry Adoption, Bureau of Consular Affairs, US Department of State, https://travel.state.gov/ content/dam/aa/pdfs/fy2014_annual_report.pdf.

73 *Congressional Coalition Adoption Institute* Congressional Coalition on Adoption Institute Facts & Statistics, http://www.cca institute.org/index.php?option=com_content&view=category &layout=blog&id=25&Itemid=43.

73 *children in foster care* The AFCARS (Adoption and Foster Care Analysis and Reporting System) Report. US Department of Health

and Human Services, Administration for Children and Families, http://www.acf.hhs.gov/sites/default/files/cb/afcarsreport22 .pdf.

75 *adult family members were involved* Lisa Westrich and Karen Strobe, "A Study of Family Engagement in Redwood City Community Schools," John W. Gardner Center for Youth and Their Communities, http://jgc.stanford.edu/resources/reports/Family EngagementIssueBrief2013.pdf.

75 *effective family engagement programs* Anne T. Henderson and Karen L. Mapp, "A New Wave of Evidence: The Impact of School, Family, and Community Connections on Student Achievement," National Center for Family & Community Connections with Schools, 2002, http://files.eric.ed.gov/fulltext/ED536946.pdf.

78 *"Review forms and regulations . . ."* Katharine Green, Melody McAllister, and Shannon Metcalf, "Divorce: Recommendations for Parents and Teachers," http://www.education.udel.edu/wp-content /uploads/2013/01/Divorce.pdf.

79 *email I sent her* Personal email correspondence with Jo Carrigan.

85 *The Family Tree* "The History of Family Trees," Mocavo.com. http://learn.mocavo.com/getting-started/the-history-of-family -trees.

86 *Family Montessori of Lebanon in Ohio.* Personal conversation with Erica Nichols.

Chapter 4.
We Will Get Through This Together

91 *grief may be a response* "What Is Grief?" Mayo Clinic Patient and Visitor Guide, http://www.mayoclinic.org/patient-visitor-guide support-groups/what-is-grief.

92 *dealing with that grief* "Grief, Mourning, and Bereavement, Coping with the Loss of a Loved One," American Cancer Society, http://www.cancer.org/treatment/treatmentsandsideeffects/ emotionalsideeffects/griefandloss/coping-with-the-loss-of-a-loved -one-intro-to-grief-mourning-bereavement.

92 *George Bonanno* Emily Esfahani Smith, "In Grief, Try Personal Rituals," *Atlantic*, March 14, 2014, http://www.theatlantic.com/ health/archive/2014/03/in-grief-try-personalrituals/284397/.

93 *additional periods of grieving* Linda Goldman, *Great Answers to Difficult Questions about Death* (Jessica Kingsley Publications, 2009).

94 *responses of the grieving child* "Helping the Grieving Student: A Guide for Teachers," The Dougy Center: National Center for Grieving Children & Families. http://tmsd.mb.ca/Crisis%20Plan/Section%207/7-A%20Helping%20the%20Grieving%20Student.pdf.

96 *how many children experience grief* "Did You Know? Children and Grief Statistics," Children's Grief Awareness Day, http://www.childrensgriefawarenessday.org/cgad2/pdf/griefstatistics.pdf.

96 *". . . a parent in prison."* "Collateral Costs: Incarceration's Effect on Economic Mobility," The Pew Charitable Trusts Research & Analysis, http://www.pewtrusts.org/en/research-and-analysis/reports/0001/01/01/collateralcosts.

96 *entering into foster care* Elise Foley, "Deportation Separated Thousands of U.S.-Born Children from Parents in 2013,' *Huffington Post*, June 26, 2014, http://www.huffingtonpost.com/2014/06/25/parents-deportation_n_5531552.html.

96 *". . . unauthorized immigrant parent . . ."* "Unauthorized Immigrants: Who They Are and What the Public Thinks," Pew Research Center, http://www.pewresearch.org/key-data-points/immigration/.

97 *divorce of their parents* Hal Arkowitz and Scott O. Lillienfeld, "Is Divorce Bad for Children?" *Scientific American Mind*, March 1, 2013, http://www.scientificamerican.com/article/is-divorce-bad-for-children/.

98 *divorce and separation can elicit* Carl E. Pickhardt, "The Impact of Divorce on Adolescents and Young Children," *Psychology Today*, Surviving (Your Child's) Adolescence, December 19, 2011, https://www.psychologytoday.com/blog/surviving-your-childs-adolescence/201112/the-impact-divorce-young-children-and-adolescents.

98 *a child's ability to learn* Hyun Sik Kim, "Consequences of Parental Divorce for Child Development," *American Sociological Review*, June 2011, http://www.asanet.org/images/journals/docs/pdf/asr/Jun11ASRFeature.pdf.

98 *an adoptive child's experience* Personal conversation with Rachael Burnett Daugherty.

100 *three roles for educators* Andrea Ruth Hopkins, "Children and Grief: The Role of the Early Childhood Educator," *Young Children,* January 2002.

100 *". . . present with grieving students . . ."* Linda Goldman, *Great Answers to Difficult Questions about Death* (Jessica Kingsley Publications, 2009).

102 *Difficult Question about Death* Linda Goldman, *Great Answers to Difficult Questions about Death* (Jessica Kingsley Publications, 2009).

105 *"Children know more than we think . . ."* "About Childhood Grief," National Alliance for Grieving Children, http://children grieve.org/about-childhood-grief.

109 *". . . preventing suicide."* "When Death Impacts Your School," The Dougy Center, National Center for Grieving Children & Families, http://www.dougy.org/grief-resources/death-impacts-your-school/.

112 *In My Classroom, Tara Seekins* Personal conversation with Tara Seekins.

115 *Alyssa Hemmelgarn* Personal conversation with Joe and Carole Hemmelgarn, alyssacares.org.

116 *Grief and Loss Inventory* Linda Goldman, *Great Answers to Difficult Questions about Death* (Jessica Kingsley Publications, 2009).

117 *Example of Grief and Loss Inventory* Adapted from Linda Goldman, *Great Answers to Difficult Questions about Death* (Jessica Kingsley Publications, 2009).

119 *". . . more caring human beings."* Linda Goldman, *Children Also Grieve* (Jessica Kingsley Publications, 2006).

Chapter 5. When Students Are in Danger

121 *Rihanna's bruised, face* Ken Lee, "Chris Brown Charged with Two Felonies in Rihanna Beating," *People,* March 5, 2009.

123 *children received preventative services* "National Statistics on Child Abuse," National Children's Alliance, http://www .nationalchildrensalliance.org/media-room/media-kit/national -statistics-child-abuse.

123 *children who experienced maltreatment* "National Statistics on Child Abuse," National Children's Alliance, http://www

.nationalchildrensalliance.org/media-room/media-kit/national -statistics-child-abuse.

123 *intimate partner violence* Statistics, National Coalition Against Domestic Violence, http://www.ncadv.org/learn/statistics.

123 *will be sexually abused* Catherine Townsend, "Prevalence: 1 in 10," *Darkness to Light*, 2013, http://www.d2l.org/site/c.4dICIJO kGcISE/b.8766307/k.A6B6/Prevalence_1_in_10.htm.

123 *"Provide educators with resources . . ."* "Dating Abuse and Teen Violence," National Coalition Against Domestic Violence, https:// www.ncadv.org/files/Dating%20Abuse%20and%20Teen%20 Violence%20NCADV.pdf.

125 *experience some form of abuse* Christopher Wildeman et al., "The Prevalence of Confirmed Maltreatment Among US Children, 2004–2011," *JAMA Pediatrics*, August 2014, http://inequality.hks .harvard.edu/files/inequality/files/wildeman14b.pdf.

125 *"People who have been traumatized . . ."* Become Trauma Informed, http://www.traumainformedcareproject.org/.

126 *" . . . wired to expect danger"* Personal conversation with Dr. James Henry.

127 *". . . an empathetic teacher . . ."* Personal conversation with Jodi Grove.

128 *mandatory reporting laws* "Mandatory Reporters of Child Abuse and Neglect," Child Welfare Information Gateway, US Department of Health and Human Services, https://www.child welfare.gov/topics/systemwide/laws-policies/statutes/manda/.

128 *Safe Horizon* "Child Abuse Facts," Safe Horizon, http://www .safehorizon.org/page/child-abuse-facts-56.html.

130 *". . . disclosures often unfold gradually . . ."* "Facts and Statistics." US Department of Justice NSOPW, https://www.nsopw.gov /en-US/Education/FactsStatistics.

130 *abuse or neglect is suspected* "Child Abuse Symptoms by Mayo Clinic Staff," Mayo Clinic Patient Care and Health Info, http:// www.mayoclinic.org/diseases-conditions/child-abuse/basics/ symptoms/con-20033789.

133 *"As an ally, a teacher . . ."* Personal conversation with Wendy O. Osefo.

133 *" . . . doubled the odds of attending college."* "Benefit of a Mentor: Disadvantaged Teens Twice as Likely to Attend College,"

Science Daily, November 2009, http://www.sciencedaily.com/releases/2009/11/091104161837.htm.

134 *In My Classroom, Sara Bradbury* Personal conversation with Sara Bradbury.

136 *What My Teacher Didn't Know, Sophia's Story* Personal conversation with a participant who wishes to remain anonymous and has had her name changed here to "Sophia."

140 *a new popular song* Personal conversation with Janessa Malisani.

142 *even when it hurts to listen* Personal conversation with Rachel Bernard.

143 *"Of all professionals ..."* "Facts and Statistics," US Department of Justice NSOPW, https://www.nsopw.gov/en-US/Education/Facts Statistics.

Chapter 6. Value-Driven Classrooms

147 *something that develops as a child learns* Anne Colby et al., "A Longitudinal Study of Moral Judgment," *Monographs of the Society for Research in Child Development,* 1983.

148 *morality is care based* Care Ethics, Internet Encyclopedia of Philosophy, http://www.iep.utm.edu/care-eth/#SH1a.

149 *an inclusive term encompassing* "Partnerships in Character Education State Pilot Projects, 1995–2001 Lessons Learned," US Department of Education Office of Safe and Drug-Free Schools, http://www2.ed.gov/programs/charactered/lessons.pdf.

150 *What My Teacher Doesn't Know, Katherine Ocaranza Cortés.* Personal conversation with Katherine Ocaranza Cortés.

153 *"did not yield evidence ..."* "Efficacy of Schoolwide Programs to Promote Social and Character Development and Reduce Problem Behavior in Elementary School Children," Social and Character Development Research Consortium, US Department of Education, October 2010, https://ies.ed.gov/ncer/pubs/20112001/pdf/20112001.

153 *". . . student development and growth."* Jacques S. Benninga et al., *Character and Academics: What Good Schools Do* (Phi Delta Kappan, February 2006), http://www.fresnostate.edu/kremen/bonnercenter/documents/Character_and_Academics.

153 *"Schools that teach character education . . ."* Jessica Lahey, "The Benefits of Character Education," *Atlantic,* May 6, 2013, http: //www.theatlantic.com/national/archive/2013/05/the-benefits -of-character-education275585.

154 *". . . creating a climate for learning . . ."* Sarah D. Sparks, "Character Education Found to Fall Short in Federal Study," *Education Week,* October 21, 2010, http://www.edweek.org/ew/articles /2010/10/21/09character.h30.html.

156 *In My Classroom, Luke Morlin* Personal conversation with Luke Morlin.

160 *"collectively, the states reported . . ."* "Efficacy of Schoolwide Programs to Promote Social and Character Development and Reduce Problem Behavior in Elementary School Children," Social and Character Development Research Consortium, US Department of Education, October 2010, https://ies.ed.gov/ncer/pubs/20112001/ pdf/20112001.pdf.

161 *"character strengths and weaknesses."* Paul Tough, "What If the Secret to Success Is Failure," *New York Times Magazine,* September 14, 2011, http://www.nytimes.com/2011/09/18/magazine/ what-if-the-secret-to-success-is-failure.html?_r=0.

161 *"Students' attention should be focused . . ."* Timothy Rusnak, *An Integrated Approach to Character Education* (Thousand Oaks, CA: Corwin Press).

162 *". . . a moral climate within our schools."* Jacques S. Benninga et al., *Character and Academics: What Good Schools Do* (Phi Delta Kappan, February 2006), http://www.fresnostate.edu/ kremen/bonnercenter/documents/Character_and_Academics.pdf.

162 *Fairness and generosity* "Performance Values: Why They Matter and What Schools Can Do to Foster Their Development," Character Education Parntership, April 2008, http://www.character .org/uploads/PDFs/White_Papers/Performance_Values.pdf.

162 *three types of values* "Character Educational Interventions: Benefits for Character Traits, Behavioral, and Academic Outcomes," Institute for Educational Sciences, What Works Clearinghouse, http://ies.ed.gov/ncee/wwc/reports/character_education/abstract.asp.

163 *". . . most important lesson to emerge . . ."* "Partnerships in Character Education State Pilot Projects, 1995–2001 Lessons Learned,"

US Department of Education Office of Safe and Drug-Free Schools, http://www2.ed.gov/programs/charactered/lessons.pdf.

163 *"What I saw emerging . . ."* Sarah D. Sparks, "Character Education Found to Fall Short in Federal Study," *Ed Week,* October 21, 2010, http://www.edweek.org/ew/articles/2010/10/21/09character.h30.html.

165 *". . . communicate effectively with others."* Joyce Thomas and Deana McDonagh, "Shared Language: Towards More Effective Communication," *Australasian Medical Journal,* January 2013, http://www.ncbi.nlm.nih.gov/pmc/articles/PMC3575067/.

167 *Character Counts Six Pillar Program* Six Pillar Rubric, Charactercounts.Org, https://charactercounts.org/pdf/Teaching-Tool_Six-Pillars-Rubric.pdf.

Chapter 7. You Got This!

173 *"Self-efficacy refers to . . ."* "Teaching Tip Sheet: Self Efficacy," American Psychological Association, http://www.apa.org/pi/aids/resources/education/self-efficacy.aspx.

174 *the ability to improve* Adapted from Carol Dweck, *Mindset: The New Psychology of Success* (New York: Random House, 2006).

174 *a student's self-talk* How Can You Change from a Fixed Mindset to a Growth Mindset? http://mindsetonline.com/changeyourmindset/firststeps/.

177 *"Pessimism is an entrenched habit . . ."* Martin Seligman, *The Optimistic Child* (New York: Houghton Mifflin, 1995).

177 *". . . emulate and duplicate behaviors . . ."* Learned Optimism: The Cup Half Full, Positive Psychology Program, http://positivepsychologyprogram.com/learned-optimism/.

178 *In My Classroom, Amy Lyon* Personal conversation with Amy Lyon.

179 *students with more grit* Claire Robertson-Kraft and Angela Lee Duckworth, "True Grit: Trait-level Perseverance and Passion for Long-term Goals Predicts Effectiveness and Retention among Novice Teachers," University of Pennsylvania, 2014, http://www.sas.upenn.edu/~duckwort/images/publications/truegrit.pdf.

183 *"When I lived in DC . . ."* Personal conversation with Angela Watson.

189 *"... strong emphasis on coteaching ..."* Personal conversation with Rob Suglia.

192 *What My Teacher Doesn't Know, Aswad Allen's Story.* Personal conversation with Aswad Allen.

194 *For important skills* Adapted from the four-point scale in *Classroom Assessments & Grading That Work* by Robert J. Marzano (Association for Supervision & Curriculum Development, 2007).

Chapter 8. *"I Can't Wait to Learn More"*

200 *"... 40 percent to 60 percent of students ..."* Adena M. Klem and James P. Connell, "Relationships Matter: Linking Teacher Support to Student Engagement and Achievement," *Journal of School Health,* September 2004, http://www.irre.org/sites/default/files/publication_pdfs/Klem_and_Connell_2004_JOSH_article_0.pdf.

200 *"... what our students want and need."* Richard Strong, Harvey F. Silver, and Amy Robinson, "Strengthening Student Engagement: What Do Students Want (and what really motivates them?)," Educational Leadership, September 1995, http://www.ascd.org/publications/educational-leadership/sept95/vol53/num01/Strengthening-Student-Engagement@-What-Do-Students-Want.aspx.

200 *student engagement* Phillip C. Schlechty, *Engaging Students: The Next Level of Working on the Work* (Jossey-Bass, 2011).

201 *"Over time, warmth ..."* Carrie J. Furrer, Ellen A. Skinner, and Jennifer R. Pitzer, "The Influence of Teacher and Peer Relationships on Students' Classroom Engagement and Everyday Motivational Resilience," National Society for the Study of Education, 2014, http://www.pdx.edu/psy/sites/www.pdx.edu.psy/files/2014-Furrer.Skinner.Pitzer%20(1).pdf.

202 *"... service learning."* K-12 Service-Learning Standards for Quality Practice, National Youth Leadership Council, 2008, https://nylcweb.files.wordpress.com/2015/10/standards_document_mar2015update.pdf.

205 *In My Classroom, Lauren Fine* Personal conversation with Lauren Fine.

208 *What My Teacher Doesn't Know, William Yakah* Personal conversation with William Yakah.

Conclusion

216 "... *capable of becoming.*" Haim G. Ginott, *Teacher and Child: A Book for Parents and Teachers* (Scribner, 1975).

216 *The Stockdale Paradox* Jim Collins, *Good to Great: Why Some Companies Make the Leap . . . And Others Don't* (Harper-Business, 2001).

217 *Our schools are more segregated by race* Richard Rothstein, "For Public Schools, Segregation Then, Segregation Since," *Economic Policy Institute,* August 27, 2013, http://www.epi.org/publication/unfinished-march-public-school-segregation/.

217 *More students in our schools than ever* Jeanne Batalova and Margie McHugh, "Number and Growth of Students in U.S. Schools in Need of English Instruction," 2009, Migration Policy Institute, August 2010, http://www.migrationpolicy.org/research/number-and-growth-students-us-schools-need-english-instruction-2009.

Index

About the Author

Photo by Chris Williams

Kyle Schwartz is a third-grade teacher. She lives in Denver, Colorado.